Transforming Financial Systems in the Baltics, Russia, and Other Countries of the Former Soviet Union

Transforming Financial Systems in the Baltics, Russia, and Other Countries of the Former Soviet Union

Editors
Malcolm Knight
Arne B. Petersen
Robert T. Price

International Monetary Fund

Production: IMF Graphics Section
Cover design and figures: In-Ok Yoon
Typesetting: Choon Lee

Library of Congress Cataloging-in-Publication Data

Transforming financial systems in the Baltics, Russia, and other countries of the former Soviet Union / editors Malcolm Knight, Arne B. Petersen, Robert T. Price.
p. cm.
ISBN 1-55775-798-4

1. Finance—Former Soviet republics. 2. Bank and banking, Central—Former Soviet republics. I. Knight, Malcolm D. (Malcolm Donald), 1944– . II. Petersen, Arne B. III. Price Robert T.
HG186.F6T7 1999
332.1'0947—dc21 99-25822
CIP

Price: $24.50

Address orders to:
International Monetary Fund, Publication Services
700 19th Street, N.W., Washington D.C. 20431, U.S.A.
Telephone: (202) 623-7430
Telefax: (202) 623-7201
E-mail: publications@imf.org
Internet: http://www.imf.org

Foreword

Over the past seven years, the IMF, in cooperation with 23 industrial country central banks and the major international and regional institutions, has been engaged in a concerted effort to strengthen central banking operations and banking sector soundness in the Baltic countries, Russia, and other countries of the former Soviet Union. It is worth noting that, despite the financial turmoil that erupted in Russia in August 1998, with adverse repercussions for the region, many of these countries have made significant progress in restructuring their economic and financial systems.

In 1991, the Baltics, Russia, and other countries of the former Soviet Union set out on the road to establishing market economies by liberalizing prices, dismantling the instruments of central planning, and initiating a process of fundamental structural reforms. Since then, these 15 countries have taken substantial steps toward achieving macroeconomic stabilization, and are well advanced in many areas of the transformation to market economies. In particular, considerable progress has been made in developing market-oriented financial structures.

Given the magnitude of the task involved in this transformation, it was clear at the outset of the process that these 15 countries would need significant financial assistance and advice to carry the process to successful completion within a reasonable time period. The IMF has at various times extended its financial support to most of the countries involved, and has engaged in an ongoing dialogue with country authorities on a wide range of macroeconomic and structural issues. The World Bank and regional and bilateral donors have also extended significant financial assistance and advice. This volume focuses more narrowly on progress achieved in the area of market-oriented central bank and financial system reforms. This has been the focus of a special cooperative effort by which, under a Group of Seven mandate, 23 central banks agreed in early 1992 to cooperate with the IMF to provide intensive technical advice to the new central banks to help develop their capability to operate efficiently in all the main central banking areas.

The Monetary and Exchange Affairs Department (MAE) of the IMF has coordinated the work of the cooperating central banks in providing advice to the transition countries on the measures needed to attain the broad goals in the financial sector that I have outlined. The program has involved several components, including regular MAE technical assistance missions to most of the countries concerned, with participation by experts from the cooperating central banks; targeted follow-up visits; the placement of long-term resident advisors—including experts from the cooperating central banks; workshops on specific topics, with the participation of cooperating central bank experts; and training activities for the staffs of the respective central banks. The expertise and staff resources devoted to providing this assistance and advice have been considerable—about 116 staff years to date. Of this total, experts from the cooperating central banks contributed an impressive four-fifths of the total, or 94 staff years, with the remainder or 22 staff years coming from the IMF.

The material for this book was prepared in May 1998, and it therefore does not capture the impact of the recent turmoil in Russia. Nevertheless, in spite of the current uncertainties, the book's conclusions remain valid. I believe it is important not to lose sight of the notable progress that has been achieved since the intensive period of central bank reforms began in the Baltics, Russia, and other countries of the former Soviet Union in early 1992.

On the inflation and output fronts there have been major achievements. Inflation rates in most countries have declined steadily since 1992, reaching single or low double digits in many cases, while growth resumed in 1997 in 13 of the 15 countries for the first time since reforms began. Of course, progress has not been uniform across countries. Those countries that succeeded early on in lowering inflation by decisively reducing their domestic financial imbalances and proceeded rapidly to implement comprehensive structural reforms have benefited most in terms of output growth and exchange rate stability. These developments, in turn, have created a stronger basis for a continued deepening of structural reforms throughout the economy, including in the financial system. By contrast, those countries where restrained financial policies have been implemented less consistently, and where structural reforms have been embraced apprehensively, have experienced more difficulty in achieving stability—and in some cases have made less progress in realizing the structural transformation. Russia's performance on inflation and growth is suffering because of the recent turmoil. The same is true to a lesser extent for some other countries in the region. Nevertheless, with a strengthening of fiscal and monetary policies and a persistent application of market-oriented reforms, developments should return to the positive trend.

During the period covered here—from early 1992 to May 1998—most of the 15 countries under review demonstrated a strong and consistent commitment to undertaking deep financial sector reforms. From the outset, they adopted the broad goal of transforming their financial systems from the monobank structure of the Soviet era to a two-tiered financial system, anchored by an independent central bank presiding over a system in which interest rates and exchange rates were market-determined and commercial banks transacted business on a competitive basis. Important elements in this transformation included the development of active government securities markets and interbank markets dealing in short-term, liquid funds and foreign exchange. A further goal has been the creation of secondary markets in which banking system liquidity could be managed by the central bank through open market operations using indirect monetary policy instruments. Also important have been the reforms of the central bank lender-of-last-resort facilities, including the development of collateralized standing facilities. Finally, the design and implementation of central bank reform in the areas of banking supervision, payment systems, and central bank accounting systems have been key elements in meeting the broad objectives.

Recent developments have underscored the importance of maintaining a sound banking system, and more work is clearly needed here. The development of a well-functioning securities market has unfortunately suffered an abrupt setback in Russia, demonstrating the need to back up sound monetary policies and procedures with appropriate fiscal policies and far-reaching structural reforms in other areas. There is now a need to restore investor confidence that has been severely weakened by Russia's unilateral decision to restructure domestic debt obligations. Nevertheless, many of the basic elements of a successful structural transformation are still in place in Russia to serve as the foundation for a return to improved economic performance—provided, of course, that broad-based support can be found for carrying them through.

From 1992 to 1998, regular joint meetings of both technical assistance donor institutions and recipient central banks were held in Basle at the Bank for International Settlements (BIS). These meetings provided a useful occasion for technical assistance providers and recipients to review the progress and effectiveness of the IMF-coordinated technical assistance program, and to plan ahead for further assistance. One conclusion from these meetings was that although the financial reform process is far from complete, there are clear indications it has been exerting a favorable effect on the implementation of monetary and financial policies throughout the region. Nonetheless, further efforts will be needed to improve overall banking system soundness in most countries. Technical assistance will continue to be provided, both by MAE and bilaterally by the cooperating central banks.

This volume was originally prepared as one of the background papers for the eleventh, and final, coordination meeting held in Basle, May 11–12, 1998. It has benefited from the substantial input of the central banks of the 15 countries covered by the survey, including their responses to a comprehensive questionnaire on which the tables in Chapter 8 are based. The report highlights the substantial progress achieved by the central banks of most of the 15 countries and the catalytic role these institutions have played in the overall development of their financial markets. To assess the technical assistance effort and provide countries with a way of determining the appropriate sequencing of further reforms, as well as to assist both recipient and donor central banks and institutions in identifying priorities for further technical assistance, the MAE staff has attempted to rank the countries' progress up to May 1998 in the key central banking areas and the financial system as a whole. These rankings are for technical assistance purposes only, and should not be viewed as an assessment of the countries' overall macroeconomic and financial policy stance.

The IMF staff and I would like to express our gratitude for the joint efforts of all cooperating central banks and international institutions that have been involved since this program of technical assistance to the central banks of the Baltics, Russia, and other countries of the former Soviet Union began. It is evident that this reform process has been an enormous task, rife with complexities. The challenges could not have been met without the extensive cooperation of the 23 central banks and financial institutions providing the technical assistance, together with the commitment of the participating countries to achieve their overall objective of establishing market-based economies. It has been a task clearly beyond the resources and capabilities of any one institution. Although the work is not yet completed—as has been dramatically demonstrated by recent events—the overall coordinated technical assistance program has been a very successful effort, both for recipients and donors. Most of all, the central banks of the Baltics, Russia, and other countries of the former Soviet Union are to be commended for embracing challenging reforms during this period. Finally, we are all most grateful to the BIS for its valued assistance in organizing the high-level coordination meetings that have been held in Basle over the past several years.

Stanley Fischer
First Deputy Managing Director
International Monetary Fund

Acknowledgments

The editors of this book would like to express their thanks to the central banks and international institutions that participated in the meetings for their comments and for the information they made available to the IMF for this book. Ms. Elizabeth Handel and Ms. Charmion O'Connor deserve much of the credit for making the production of the initial manuscript as smooth and efficient as possible. Natalie Baumer edited an earlier version of the manuscript, and Ms. Liliane Yomekpe helped in revising the manuscript for publication. Jeff Hayden of the External Relations Department edited the final manuscript and coordinated its production.

Contents

1

Overview

Malcolm Knight, Arne B. Petersen, and Robert T. Price

For the past six years, the central banks of the Baltics, Russia, and other countries of the former Soviet Union have undertaken ambitious programs of reform.[1] The reforms have focused first on stabilizing monetary policy and then on achieving a market-based determination of interest and exchange rates. The reform of central bank operating procedures has been a key piece of the program. Central banks in the 15 countries have been encouraged to manage banking liquidity through market operations with indirect instruments. There have also been closely coordinated reforms to foster foreign exchange markets, interbank money markets, government securities markets, and to strengthen various central bank functions, including the payment system, central bank accounting and internal audit, and banking supervision and restructuring. This volume examines the progress the 15 countries have made in transforming their financial systems, and highlights the substantial progress achieved by central banks in most of the countries.

The chapters were originally prepared as sections of a background paper for the eleventh and final coordination meeting (May 1998) of 23 cooperating central banks and other major and international and regional institutions that have been providing technical assistance to the central banks of the 15 countries since early 1992. The donors have met regularly since 1992 to evaluate the progress of reforms, assess the effectiveness of technical assistance activities, and review staff resource commitments under the technical assistance pro-

[1]The Baltics, Russia, and other countries of the former Soviet Union include Armenia, Azerbaijan, Belarus, Estonia, Georgia, Kazakhstan, Kyrgyz Republic, Latvia, Lithuania, Moldova, Russia, Tajikistan, Turkmenistan, Ukraine, and Uzbekistan.

gram.[2] At the 1996 high-level coordination meeting, participants agreed that most of the central banks in the 15 countries were reaching the stage where comprehensive technical assistance and advice from multilateral and bilateral donors on central banking functions were no longer needed. Therefore, the group decided to target the 1998 meeting as the final or "sunset" meeting of high-level representatives. Nevertheless, the group also recognized that there would be a continuing and substantial need for more specialized technical assistance in a number of areas, and that a few countries would require close support. Thus, there might be a need for a new, streamlined framework for future coordination efforts. This volume discusses remaining issues and points to areas where further reform is needed.

The structure of this book is similar to background studies prepared for previous years' coordination meetings.[3] Specifically, the book reviews the central banks' progress during 1997 in moving closer to achievement of their medium-term objectives, as well as the technical assistance and support that have fostered this process. In addition, it also evaluates more broadly the cumulative progress that has been made since the start of reform in the early 1990s, and attempts to assess both the scope and sequencing of further reform measures needed to help each country meet international standards or best practices.

As in previous years, this background study attempts to rank, on a scale of I to III, the degree of progress that each country has achieved in the main central banking areas surveyed here. A ranking of (I) signifies limited progress; (II), moderate progress; and (III), substantial progress. An overall ranking based on the individual rankings for the key functional areas is also included. The same caveat as in previous years' ranking exercises applies—measuring the rate of progress necessarily involves qualitative assessments, and the assigned rankings must therefore be treated with appropriate caution. Countries judged to have made "substantial progress" in financial system reform compared to their peer group in many cases still have further work to do in order to conform to best international practices and standards. Nevertheless, the rankings provided here

[2]The cooperating central banks include those of Australia, Austria, Belgium, Canada, Denmark, Finland, France, Germany, Iceland, Ireland, Israel, Italy, Japan, the Netherlands, New Zealand, Norway, Portugal, Spain, Sweden, Switzerland, Turkey, the United Kingdom, and the United States.

[3]The background papers for the 1996 meeting were published in V. Sundararajan, Arne B. Petersen, and Gabriel Sensenbrenner, *Central Bank Reform in the Transition Economies* (Washington: International Monetary Fund, 1997). The background papers from the 1997 meeting were collected in Malcolm Knight and others, *Central Bank Reforms in the Baltics, Russia, and Other Countries of the Former Soviet Union*, IMF Occasional Paper No. 157 (Washington: International Monetary Fund, 1997).

are intended to assist the coordinating central banks and technical assistance donors in drawing broad conclusions about the effectiveness of their past efforts, the extent of the further reform measures needed in each country, and the associated technical assistance requirements. The rankings are partly based on comprehensive questionnaires that were addressed to the authorities in all recipient countries, in conjunction with the IMF's ongoing contacts with the authorities in the course of technical assistance and other country work.

Summary of Findings in Key Functional Areas

Overall, good progress has been made in most central banking areas, although results have differed significantly among countries.

Monetary Operations and Government Securities Markets

Since 1992, most of the 15 countries reviewed in this book have made important progress toward establishing efficient market-based financial instruments, although further reforms are still needed to achieve basic goals of well-functioning, short-term interbank and government securities markets. Interest rate controls have been abolished, so that deposit and lending rates are now market-determined in most of the countries. The basic structure of interbank markets has been put in place, but liquidity in these markets remains thin in many of the countries, owing to the varying credit quality of financial institutions and the lack of trust between commercial bank counterparties, the unfamiliarity and inexperience with short-term liquidity management at commercial banks, and uncertainties surrounding payment and settlement services between banks. To address this lack of interbank development, many countries are introducing repurchase agreements as the basis for interbank trading. Primary markets for government securities have been established in most countries, although market participation in primary auctions has been mixed. The maturities of government securities remain primarily short-term, partly because of continuing concerns over inflation risk. Secondary markets in government securities have been slower to establish and develop in many countries, but there is reasonable depth and liquidity in Kazakhstan, Latvia, and Russia.

Most of the 15 countries have begun to exercise monetary control through indirect, market-based instruments. Only a few resort to direct monetary instruments and controls. Bank-by-bank credit ceilings have been eliminated in all countries, and limits on cash withdrawals by depositors are now maintained only in Turkmenistan and Uzbekistan. Directed credits, often at below-market rates, still exist in some countries (Belarus, Turkmenistan, and Uzbekistan). The design of indirect instruments and market-based central bank standing and discretionary facilities has progressed significantly in many countries, but thin interbank markets have hampered the monetary transmission mechanism, and in some cases central banks need to streamline the number of instruments and facilities used. While most of the countries are employing monetary programming techniques, the application of these methods has been hampered by deficiencies in their central bank's short-term forecasting and liquidity management techniques. This stems largely from coordination problems, both within central bank departments and between the central bank and the finance ministry or treasury, in producing accurate short-term forecasts of government cash flows.

Two of the Baltic countries—Estonia and Lithuania—operate currency board arrangements, and thus are precluded from active monetary operations. Kazakhstan, the Kyrgyz Republic, Latvia, and Russia have made the most progress overall in introducing market-based monetary policy instruments and establishing interbank and secondary markets for financial instruments.

Following the initial stages of reforms in early 1992, the combination of rapid monetary expansions, limited supplies of goods, and government controls on prices induced sharp increases in real money balances. This in turn fueled spiraling inflation rates when prices were liberalized, and the value of those balances subsequently fell from late 1992 through 1994. The first steps toward macroeconomic stabilization brought about a leveling out in the real value of monetary aggregates, albeit at levels well below those in developing countries. Dollarization, although difficult to measure, has also been a significant factor in most countries through the period since liberalization began. These circumstances have been associated with instability in money demand relationships that have hampered the application of monetary management frameworks based on standard monetary and liquidity programming techniques.

Future efforts need to focus on fostering more liquid interbank money markets and secondary markets for government securities, improving the effectiveness of monetary operations using indirect instruments, and providing more complete financial markets. The streamlining of central bank operations through fully collateralized instruments such as repurchase agreements or Lombard-type facilities, and the gradual development of more stable money demand relationships, including banks' demand for excess reserves, will enhance the monetary transmission mechanism and the implementation of medium-term policies directed toward price stability. Monetary policy, of course, is but one element that can contribute to good overall macroeconomic performance. Other supporting structural policies, in both the financial and real sectors, play crucial roles in the monetary and broader macroeconomic setting.

Foreign Exchange Markets and Official Reserves

Progress toward the efficient market-based determination of exchange rates is well advanced in most of the countries, including the areas of current account convertibility, and to a lesser extent, capital account convertibility; interbank market development; and central bank foreign exchange operations. Two-thirds of these countries are judged to have made substantial overall progress in this area. The three Baltic countries formally peg their currencies (Estonia to the deutsche mark and Lithuania to the U.S. dollar through currency board arrangements, and Latvia to the IMF's special drawing right, or SDR). Five others (Russia and Ukraine, with exchange rate bands, and Georgia, Tajikistan, and Turkmenistan) operate de facto exchange rate pegs. The remaining seven countries operate regimes with varying degrees of flexibility, from those where the exchange rate is determined mainly in the interbank market with negligible official intervention, to those where the central bank is the market-maker and sets the rate. Exchange rates have been unified in all but two countries (Uzbekistan and Turkmenistan), and all but four (Belarus, Tajikistan, Turkmenistan, and Uzbekistan) have achieved current account convertibility. Furthermore, capital accounts are relatively unrestricted in five countries (the three Baltic countries, Georgia, and Kyrgyz Republic), with gradual liberalization continuing in several others.[4] While auction mechanisms were implemented at the start of the reform process, they are gradually being phased out in favor of over-the-counter interbank trading arrangements, which decentralize the allocation of foreign exchange. Over-the-counter markets also support a variety of exchange rate regimes, from fixed to freely floating rates.

Although many of the countries have institutional arrangements in place for an efficient foreign exchange market, activity often remains thin, owing partly to counterparty concerns in the interbank foreign exchange market. Enhancing the liquidity of interbank trading remains a priority for future reform and, as in the domestic interbank money and securities markets, depends crucially on better counterparty information and more generally on strengthening banking sector soundness. Eliminating surrender requirements in those countries that have not already done so, and improving the foreign exchange payment system to minimize settlement risks, are other key elements that need to be addressed in coming years. Countries may also need assistance in developing contingency strategies to deal with volatile capital flows and the orderly liberalization of capital account transactions. Technical assistance in dealing with volatile capital

[4]In addition, Armenia's capital account is also presently unrestricted, but the regulations explicitly allow for the reintroduction of capital controls.

inflows may involve the design of flexible market-based exchange arrangements, including an exit strategy from a peg regime, and advice to enhance the coordination of monetary and exchange rate policies. These developments, which result from globalization, liberalization, and financial innovation, call for an integrated approach to technical assistance in capital account liberalization; that is, one that emphasizes the linkages between liberalization and the need for sound financial markets and institutions and appropriate macroeconomic policies.

Bank Supervision and Restructuring

The process of financial market liberalization and reform that began early in the decade was the impetus for a rapid expansion of the number of banks operating in the Baltics, Russia, and other countries of the former Soviet Union. Many banks prospered during this early period of high inflation and currency depreciation, through intermediation in relatively safe government bonds or through speculative activity in a depreciating currency, rather than through traditional banking business, which would have fostered credit extension and financial deepening. The basic legal frameworks for bank intermediation, accounting and judicial infrastructures, and banking supervision and regulatory regimes did not keep pace with this development. Large macroeconomic imbalances soon followed, and a number of banks came to the brink of insolvency in the mid-1990s. In virtually all countries under review this near collapse led to broader systemic problems in the banking sector, which will require considerable amounts of human and financial capital and technical assistance to correct. These problems in some cases will take years to address.

Consolidation and recapitalization of the banking system are now well under way in many of the countries, with almost all taking important initiatives in systemic reform, supported by much multilateral and bilateral technical cooperation. Bank restructuring, however, is not yet complete. Further enhancement to supervisory capabilities will be needed to keep pace with the financial deepening and the increases in bank intermediation that should flow from sustainable economic expansion in coming years.

Twelve of the countries have conducted broad diagnostic reviews of their banking systems as the first step toward developing comprehensive bank restructuring plans. About half the countries have adopted overall bank restructuring policies, while the others have dealt with these issues using a bank-by-bank approach. Key elements have included the strengthening of bank licensing requirements, recapitalization, both through shareholder capital and retained earnings or dividends, and, for the remaining state-owned banks, through government recapitalization or privatization plans and the tightening of provisioning rules. Through application of firm licensing and exit policies, as well as mergers, the banking system is undergoing a sizeable consolidation, resulting in a marked reduction in the number of banks. Until now, however, much of the consolidation and restructuring efforts have been directed toward smaller banks. In the near future, some countries, particularly Moldova, Russia, and Ukraine, will need to redirect these efforts toward problem banks, including the large formerly state-owned banks. While two-thirds of the countries have delegated the responsibility of dealing with problem banks to a central authority, only two (Kyrgyz Republic and Lithuania) have chosen to create asset management agencies to deal with insolvent banks.

The legal framework for effective banking supervision is now established in all 15 countries and has been supported by considerable technical cooperation over the past five years. Much progress has been made in the implementation of banking supervision standards in most of these countries; but further groundwork must be established in Belarus, Tajikistan, and Uzbekistan. Most countries have raised minimum capital requirements to acceptable levels to create new banks. At the same time, capital adequacy requirements have been considerably strengthened, although these could be further reinforced beyond the suggested minimum Basle ratios, which are designed for internationally active banks in well-established markets. Asset qualities have improved in the majority of the countries, with nonperforming loans now reported at around 10 percent of total assets on a simple average basis, although there are wide variations in the estimates across countries.

Major concerns persist about the accuracy, comparability, and quality of commercial bank accounting data in many countries—key priorities for reform. The lack of consolidated accounts and supervision on a consolidated basis according to international accounting standards (including off-balance sheet items), as well as the enhancement of off-site analysis and on-site inspection programs are other elements of banking supervision that require strengthening.

Payment System Operations and Policies

Most of the countries have made impressive strides in improving their domestic payment systems, although much remains to be done to develop diversified consumer-oriented payment services of a standard comparable to those in mature market economies. Nevertheless, more than half the countries have made substantial progress in addressing the strategic issues of payment system policy and design, and only one—Tajikistan—has lagged substantially behind. There is some evidence of the salutary effect of payment system improvements on domestic intermediation and financial deepening—as reflected in lower currency-to-GDP ratios—although of course the contributions of monetary policy and sounder banking systems are integrally involved. Central banks of the Baltics, Russia, and other countries of the former Soviet Union have themselves played a leading role in the development of payment systems, including offering clearing services. In some cases (Kazakhstan, Russia, and Ukraine), the central bank has implemented pricing policies for its services to encourage involvement of the private sector in the design, development, and management of an efficient payment system.

Good progress has been achieved in consolidating settlement accounts at the central banks, to enable commercial banks to manage their day-to-day liquidity more effectively, although in some countries banks have only achieved, or are aiming for, regional rather than national account consolidation (Georgia, Russia, and Tajikistan), while in two others (Azerbaijan and Uzbekistan), bank account holdings are still highly dispersed.

The introduction of systemic risk controls in support of financial stability has been a key element in the recent efforts of these countries. Settlement discipline has been promoted through strict limits on access to central bank credit. Such limits also play an important role in the development of well-functioning interbank markets, although trading in this area remains thin in most countries because of solvency concerns and credit tiering among commercial banks.

Where substantial progress has been made in payment system policies, technical assistance will increasingly need to focus on specialized topics of evolving systems and technology. The development of specialized large value transfer systems, which are seen as a cornerstone for broader financial market evolution, is such a topic. These transfer systems are in embryonic stages in most of the countries, many of which are planning real-time gross settlement systems, with built-in links to delivery-versus-payment systems for domestic securities markets. Real-time gross settlement systems are now operating in Kazakhstan and Belarus, and a pilot system is being tried by a limited number of Russian banks in the Moscow region. Further work remains to be done to consolidate the legal basis underlying payment system arrangements, including bankruptcy and collateral laws, and, importantly, to expedite the execution of these laws through the courts. Another important area where reform is needed is in the containment of foreign exchange settlement risks.

Central Bank Accounting and Internal Audit

Two-thirds of the countries have made substantial progress in implementing central bank accounting and audit reforms. Central banks in 11 countries—Armenia, Azerbaijan, Belarus, Estonia, Georgia, Kazakhstan, the Kyrgyz Republic, Latvia, Lithuania, Moldova, and Ukraine—have introduced, or are about to introduce, accounting systems and policies and procedures that are broadly consistent with International Accounting Standards (IAS). Much improvement has also been made toward full public disclosure of transparent accounting information, essential to building broader confidence in the financial sector. In nearly all these countries, the central banks' books have been subject to varying degrees of independent assessment by internationally recognized external auditors. Internal audit reform has occurred at a somewhat slower pace, although most countries recognize the need for improvement in this area. All countries have adopted a new chart of accounts, except Tajikistan, where a new chart is under consideration. Countries that are considered to have made moderate progress (Turkmenistan and Uzbekistan) have adopted a new chart of accounts, but these statements have not yet received a "clean" opinion by independent external auditors.

In the area of central bank accounting, the priorities for reform in the most advanced countries will be to enhance financial management control and information systems. Improvements in these two areas will permit more efficient use of central bank resources, establish policies to maintain central bank financial soundness, and allow the central bank to play a leadership role in establishing full and transparent disclosure standards, which, in turn, will promote general financial discipline in the financial system. Some countries still have gaps in their basic knowledge and application of accounting policies, including adoption of the accruals principle, valuation of assets, and the preparation of a full set of financial statements (in some cases preparation is impeded by conceptual or political obstacles to reform). Other relevant issues that will require further reform in all 15 countries, and in some instances additional specialized technical assistance, include the development and implementation of accounting policies for new financial instruments, especially off-balance sheet items; more structured staff training and development; management of new technologies and information systems; and harmonization of central bank and financial sector accounting and reporting standards.

Legislative Framework

Before 1991, the U.S.S.R. operated a monobank system in which savings were pooled and credit was allocated on the basis of centralized planning. Since 1992, all 15 countries have made considerable progress toward the creation of the legislative framework for a two-tiered banking system comprising an autonomous central bank and commercial banks that compete with each other and with other financial intermediaries. In these countries, the basic legal frameworks are now in place to enable the effective operation of a modern central bank with clear policy objectives and the political and operational autonomy to achieve those objectives. Eleven of the countries under review have made price stability the primary objective of central bank legislation, either explicitly or implicitly, through linking the currency to an anchor currency. Of the remaining countries, Azerbaijan, Russia, and Turkmenistan include price stability as one among multiple objectives, while Ukraine designates monetary or currency stability as one of its objectives.[5]

Legislative measures to ensure political and economic autonomy have also been built into laws governing central banks. The laws generally guarantee that the term of office for the central bank governor and for board members is longer than the election cycle, and in some cases include a double-veto arrangement for appointments. Provisions to assure the financial soundness of the central bank, including clear rules on the transfer of central bank profits and the responsibility of the government to recapitalize the bank in the event of losses are also provided. As a counterpart to the provisions granting central bank autonomy, provisions are also imposed on the central bank to ensure that it is accountable to the government and the public for its policies and actions. A key element of accountability is the publication of regular reports that make the policies and operations of the central bank more transparent, including officially audited financial statements that conform to IAS.[6] While most central bank laws in the 15 countries include these basic elements, Estonia, Latvia, Lithuania, and Ukraine are currently examining ways to strengthen aspects of central bank autonomy and accountability. Belarus is also reviewing its central bank legislation, although it appears that some current proposals would weaken the autonomy of its central bank, the National Bank of Belarus.

Much of the legislative framework required for the efficient allocation of savings and the operation of financial markets is beyond the immediate purview of the central bank. The central bank has no influence over such basic laws as those governing property rights and contracts, bankruptcy, and the use of collateral, including the registration of liens. Furthermore, the laws that underpin financial markets and transactions must be supported and enforced through an efficient judicial process. These basic institutional and legal measures, once firmly established, will clarify the

[5]A revised central bank law that includes price stability as a primary objective has been prepared for parliamentary discussion in Ukraine.

[6]IAS are promulgated by the International Accounting Standards Committee, composed of over 120 professional accounting bodies in 91 countries. The organization establishes the standards for the presentation of financial statements.

rights and obligations of counterparties to financial transactions. The confidence in market-based transactions will contribute to domestic financial deepening and currency stability, foster the establishment of fully market-determined interest rates through more liquid financial instruments and complete capital markets, and facilitate the application of indirect instruments of monetary policy. Other key impediments remain, however, including weaknesses in the payment system, unclear accounting standards, and bank unsoundness, that will slow the pace of overall financial market development to varying degrees in each of the countries.

Country Rankings

While all of the 15 countries covered in this book seek a fundamental transformation of their economic and financial systems over the medium term, inevitably, during the last six years, progress in the various key areas of central banking reforms has differed across countries. To help countries in determining the appropriate sequencing of further reforms, and to assist both recipient and donor central banks and institutions in identifying priorities for further technical assistance, the IMF has updated its rankings of each country's progress in the key areas of reform and for each country's financial system as a whole.

Countries are ranked by degree of progress: (I) limited, (II) moderate, and (III) substantial. The rankings are intended to provide a rough assessment of the relative progress made by each country from the end of 1991 to the present. Analogous exercises were conducted for three previous coordination meetings of technical assistance providers (1994–96), but an additional category covering central bank legislation has been included this year. Because of additional information and the methodology employed, including the additional legislative category, the individual and overall rankings presented in this report may not be strictly comparable to the earlier ones. In particular, a country may have registered steady progress since the earlier reviews, but may still be ranked in the same category. Moreover, a lower ranking would not necessarily indicate backtracking by the country, but might reflect lower-than-average progress compared with the peer group.

Of course, measuring this medium-term progress necessarily involves qualitative assessments, especially as to how far each central bank has moved toward implementing new market-based instruments and procedures of monetary policy, and how financial markets have responded. The assigned rankings must therefore be treated only as a rough indicator of areas that should receive priority in order to maintain the momentum of structural transformation in each country. A substantial ranking (III) does not imply that the country has fully achieved international standards or

Table 1.1. Progress on Central Banking Reforms: Country Rankings, 1997

	Central Bank Legislation	Monetary Operations and Debt Management	Foreign Exchange Operations	Banking Supervision	Bank Restructuring	Payments System	Central Bank Accounting and Audit	Overall Ranking
Armenia	III	II	III	III	III	II	III	III
Azerbaijan	II	I	II	II	II	II	III	II
Belarus	I	I	I	I	I	III	III	I
Estonia	III	*	III	III	III	III	III	III
Georgia	III	II	III	III	III	II	III	III
Kazakhstan	II	III	III	III	III	III	III	III
Kyrgyz Republic	III	III	III	III	III	III	III	III
Latvia	II	III	III	III	III	III	III	III
Lithuania	III	*	III	III	II	III	III	III
Moldova	III	II	III	III	III	II	III	III
Russia	II	III	III	III	II	III	II	III
Tajikistan	II	I	I	I	I	I	I	I
Turkmenistan	II	I	I	II	I	II	II	I
Ukraine	I	II	III	II	II	III	III	II
Uzbekistan	II	II	I	II	II	II	II	II

Note: *Denotes currency board arrangements; the rankings denote the following: (I) limited progress; (II) moderate progress; and (III) substantial progress.

best practices in that area, and further actions, and possibly technical assistance, may continue to be needed. Finally, the rankings for each country reflect the pace of structural changes toward a market-based financial system and are not intended as an assessment of countries' overall macroeconomic and financial policy stance.

The rankings listed in Table 1.1 summarize the progress made up to the end of 1997 in seven major functional areas: central bank legislation; monetary operations and government securities markets; foreign exchange operations and official international reserve management; banking supervision; bank restructuring; payment systems; and central bank accounting and internal audit. They are based on technical criteria outlined later in this book. The overall ranking is derived by aggregating those in each individual category. Specifically, countries that have at least four ratings of III and no rating of I have been accorded an overall rating of III. Countries that have three or more ratings of I have been given an overall rating of I. The other countries have received a rating of II. Each of the functional areas is given equal weight.

Central banks in the Baltics, Russia, and the other countries of the former Soviet Union have recognized that implementation of the key central banking reforms discussed in this book will improve monetary control, strengthen financial intermediation, and lead to improved overall macroeconomic performance. During the past few years, the reforms undertaken in these countries have been instrumental in bringing about price and foreign exchange market stabilization, although for some countries, the resumption of steady economic growth still lies ahead. It is not an easy matter to link reforms and improved economic performance with precision, but several recent empirical studies point to broad linkages between progress in structural reform and improved economic performance.[7]

[7]These include: J. Sachs and W.T. Woo, "Structural Factors in the Economic Reforms of China, Eastern Europe, and the Former Soviet Union," *Economic Policy: A European Forum*, Vol. 9, No. 4 (April, 1994), pp. 101–45; M. Selowsky and R. Martin, "Policy Performance and Output Growth in Transition Economies," *American Economic Review, Papers and Proceedings*, Vol. 87 (May, 1997), pp. 349–53; and E. Hernández-Catá, "Liberalization and the Behavior of Output During the Transition from Plan to Market," *Staff Papers*, Vol. 44, No. 4 (December, 1997), pp. 405–29.

2

Monetary Operations and Government Securities Markets

Eduardo Levy-Yeyati

Country experiences with monetary operations and government securities markets have been highly diverse, but a general pattern seems to have emerged since early 1992: most countries have moved toward more central bank operational autonomy and increased reliance on indirect instruments and on market-based interest rates. In addition, with few exceptions, reforms have led to a slow but sustained growth of the interbank and government securities markets. The sequencing of reforms has varied widely across countries, because of different political and macroeconomic conditions, and faster developments in one central banking area have not always been accompanied by similar progress in others (Table 2.1).

Recent Developments

The following sections review specific steps taken by central banks during 1997 to enhance the monetary transmission mechanism through the use of indirect instruments, and also survey the important changes since the onset of reforms.

Monetary Policy Framework

Since 1992, the enactment of central bank laws in the Baltics, Russia, and other countries of the former Soviet Union has provided most of the countries' central banks with a considerable degree of formal autonomy to carry out an independent monetary policy.[1] Central bank legislation has

[1]Exceptions are Belarus, Turkmenistan, and Uzbekistan.

Table 2.1. Country Rankings in Monetary Operations and Government Securities Markets

Rankings	I Limited Progress	II Moderate Progress	III Substantial Progress
Central bank facilities			
Standing, collateralized (Lombard, rediscount), and discretionary (open market operations)	Azerbaijan Belarus Tajikistan Turkmenistan	Armenia Georgia Uzbekistan	Kazakhstan Kyrgyz Republic Latvia Moldova Russia Ukraine
Operating framework			
Use of monetary programming and short-term liquidity forecasting	Tajikistan Turkmenistan Uzbekistan	Armenia Azerbaijan Belarus Georgia Latvia Moldova Ukraine	Kazakhstan Kyrgyz Republic Russia
Market development			
Interbank money market and secondary market for government securities	Armenia Azerbaijan Belarus Tajikistan Turkmenistan	Georgia Kyrgyz Republic Moldova Ukraine Uzbekistan	Kazakhstan Latvia Russia
Overall ranking	Azerbaijan Belarus Tajikistan Turkmenistan	Armenia Georgia Moldova Ukraine Uzbekistan	Kazakhstan Kyrgyz Republic Latvia Russia

Note: Estonia and Lithuania have currency board arrangements and thus do not actively manage banking system liquidty. Hence, they are excluded from this classification.

also provided a clear objective for monetary policy—price stability. This target is set out in the recently enacted central bank laws of Armenia, Azerbaijan, Georgia, the Kyrgyz Republic, Russia, Tajikistan, and Uzbekistan.[2] Over the same period, central bank credit to the government has declined steadily, as governments have moved toward market financing through the issue of government debt, and some countries have explicitly prohibited central bank lending to the government (Estonia and

[2]Other aspects of central bank legislation are discussed in Chapter 7.

Lithuania, which operate currency boards, and Kazakhstan and Kyrgyz Republic).

At present, most countries surveyed in this report are using monetary programming techniques and adopting monetary operations to foster market development and monetary control. Most countries have established medium-term operating frameworks and targets for monetary policy that follow performance criteria for central bank balance sheets developed under IMF-sponsored macroeconomic adjustment programs.[3] Success on this front has been mixed, as changing macroeconomic conditions often conspired against the formulation of monetary policy based on stable long-run relationships between monetary aggregates and economic activity.

Less progress has generally been achieved in short-term forecasting and liquidity management, which has hampered the coordination of a mix of indirect monetary policy instruments. Day-to-day liquidity management has also been hindered by limited coordination between operations in the domestic money market and foreign exchange operations (Belarus, Moldova, Russia, and Turkmenistan), and difficulties in forecasting certain balance sheet items such as government cash positions (Georgia, Kazakhstan, Latvia, Tajikistan, and Turkmenistan) and net other items. More important, the lack of fully developed interbank and secondary government securities markets affects the functioning of the monetary transmission mechanism, thereby limiting the ability of central banks to link short-term liquidity management with the medium-term objectives established in the monetary program. These deficiencies have tended to limit the scope for more active liquidity management through the use of indirect instruments. Nevertheless, substantial progress has been achieved in the Kyrgyz Republic, Russia, and, to a lesser extent, Kazakhstan.

Markets and Interest Rate Management

While interbank money markets are in place in most of the 15 countries and have begun to play a role in redistributing liquidity among financial institutions, activity in many cases remains limited. After suffering setbacks in 1995 and 1996 because of banking crises or concerns regarding counterparty risk, Kazakhstan, Latvia, Lithuania, and Russia resumed the development of interbank money markets in 1997. This was due in part to a decline in credit risks as unsound banks were liquidated or reorganized and supervision was strengthened (Kyrgyz Republic), and to a gradual

[3]Of the 15 countries in the region, only Belarus, Lithuania, Turkmenistan, and Uzbekistan do not currently have programs supported by IMF financial arrangements.

buildup of the stock of usable collateral (Kyrgyz Republic and Moldova). The interbank market is also increasingly used for liquidity management in Armenia, although market growth has been hindered by bank solvency problems. In most cases, inadequate legislation on collateral remains an obstacle, and the lack of accurate information to banks on settlement balances in Georgia, Kazakhstan, Russia, and Tajikistan has prevented these countries from using the market for end-of-day funding operations. In Russia, the lack of settlement balance information was a serious hindrance for end-of-day interbank activity, although the situation improved in February 1997 when the central bank introduced multiple clearings. Russia has also experienced market segmentation (both geographically and across market participants), which has been a further constraint on the efficient redistribution of liquidity. In Turkmenistan, interbank market activity remains stagnant, despite improvements in the timeliness of settlement balance account information.

Regarding the primary market for government securities, the share of government deficits financed through the issue of treasury bills has increased steadily. Primary issuance of bills, however, has seldom been used by the central banks for short-term liquidity management. In some cases—Armenia, Kazakhstan, and the Kyrgyz Republic—the stock of government securities in the central bank's balance sheet has been built up by securitizing existing government debt and government credit lines. To compensate for the lack of monetary instruments used to absorb liquidity, central banks in Belarus, Estonia, Kazakhstan, and Uzbekistan have issued central bank securities and in Armenia, Latvia, and Russia have offered central bank term deposits on a temporary basis. Interest rates on these instruments are determined at auctions, except in Latvia and Russia, where the rates on central bank deposits are administered. The primary market is active in all countries except Estonia and Tajikistan, and volumes outstanding are growing. Since the central banks of Estonia and Lithuania operate under a currency board agreement, they do not engage in active liquidity management. Tajikistan has plans to introduce treasury bills in the near future. Two countries, Azerbaijan and Uzbekistan, began to issue treasury bills in 1996, while Georgia began to auction treasury bills in August 1997. Turkmenistan issues a limited amount of treasury bills, but not in an auction format.

In the primary issues of securities, the central bank usually acts as the government agent and the ministry of finance decides on the timing, volume, and cutoff prices. There has been a lengthening in the maturity of the securities issued in the more established markets as inflation has declined. In a number of countries—Armenia, Kazakhstan, Latvia, Lithuania, Moldova, Russia, and Ukraine—nonresident investors strongly influence demand.

The central banks in Kazakhstan, Latvia, Ukraine, Russia, and, more recently, Armenia, Lithuania, and Moldova have begun to conduct transactions in the secondary market for government securities. Over-the-counter secondary market trading was recently introduced in Armenia and Lithuania. During 1997, the Bank of Lithuania reintroduced repurchase operations in treasury bills, while the Central Bank of Armenia initiated such operations in treasury bonds after an earlier, experimental use of similar operations in bills. Ukraine also conducts limited repurchase operations for liquidity management purposes. Open market operations in the secondary market still play a limited role in liquidity management owing to a lack of market depth and, to a certain extent, the absence of an institutional framework for conducting repurchase agreements. Many of the countries have favored the implementation of electronic trading systems to reduce counterparty risk and to increase the transparency of operations in markets where participants lack a meaningful track record and information is scarce. The Kyrgyz Republic installed an electronic trading system in April 1998, and Moldova had plans to implement one in 1998. In other countries, secondary markets are small or nonexistent, owing in part to the recent move to market-based monetary policy (Armenia[4] and Azerbaijan), or because of the absence of a meaningful primary treasury bill market (Turkmenistan). The absence of adequate systems for payments, book entry, or information linking market participants, and uneven tax treatment of earnings from securities portfolio, as in Lithuania, Moldova, and, until 1997, Armenia, also limit market development.

Controls on deposit and lending rates have been eliminated in most countries. Kazakhstan abolished its indirect control on interest rates in 1996; Ukraine eliminated the mandatory link between lending rates and the refinance rate in 1995; and Georgia liberalized prudential limits on the mobilization of household deposits in January 1997. Belarus, however, restricts lending rates on loans using central bank funds from exceeding the refinance rate plus a pre-set margin; the country eliminated minimum rates on deposits in 1995, but reintroduced them in April 1997. Uzbekistan maintains a limit on lending rates at 150 percent of the refinance rate. In 1996 and 1997, Turkmenistan loaned a substantial amount to selected industries and agriculture by presidential decree at rates below its central bank refinance rate. Some countries have linked the refinance rate to market-based interest rates. In Azerbaijan and Moldova the refinance rate is linked to the credit auction rate, and in the Kyrgyz Republic to the treasury bill rate. In other cases, the refinance rate is determined on

[4]Armenia introduced repurchase agreements on a small scale in 1996, followed by more significant measures in early 1998.

the basis of the expected inflation rate, with the aim of keeping it positive in real terms, as in Kazakhstan, Tajikistan, Turkmenistan, and Ukraine. This approach is also followed in Belarus, but it has relatively little impact since most credit (almost 90 percent) is extended at a subsidized rate below the refinance rate.

Instruments and Monetary Policy Implementation

Direct instruments are now seldom used in the 15 countries. Bank-by-bank credit ceilings have been phased out in all cases, including Tajikistan in 1997. Turkmenistan and Uzbekistan are the last countries to impose limitations on cash withdrawals. While most countries have lifted controls on interest rates, Belarus and Turkmenistan currently use directed credits with subsidized interest rates set below their refinance rates on a regular basis, and in Uzbekistan directed credits are granted for crop financing in specific situations.

Reserve requirements have been an important monetary policy instrument in the countries under review, and compliance has improved over time, including in Belarus, Georgia, Kazakhstan, and Russia. In Russia, compliance had been particularly weak in 1995, but it improved in 1996 as a result of regulations allowing the central bank unilaterally to transfer balances of delinquent banks from their correspondent accounts to reserve accounts. Most countries have chosen or recently moved to uniform ratios for different maturities and currencies.[5] Countries with nonuniform requirements—Belarus, Uzbekistan, and, until February 1998, Russia—typically set lower ratios for foreign currency deposits. Russia has made several changes in its reserve requirements since 1997 and in early 1998 introduced a uniform 11 percent reserve requirement for all commercial banks. Uzbekistan also maintains different ratios for different categories of banks. Meanwhile, Belarus has established a reserve ratio that is differentiated by maturity, ranges from 5 percent to 17 percent, and applies to both domestic and foreign currency deposits of up to one year. Lithuania is another country that differentiates by deposit maturity. Most countries stipulate that reserve requirements on both domestic and foreign currency deposits be met in the domestic currency.[6] The

[5]Ratios vary from 8 percent in Latvia and Moldova to 20 percent in the Kyrgyz Republic. Tajikistan introduced uniform reserve requirements in January 1997; Ukraine moved to a uniform reserve requirement of 11 percent in April 1997; and Armenia reintroduced a uniform reserve ratio of 8 percent in August 1997.

[6]This is in line with the IMF's Monetary and Exchange Affairs Department (MAE) recommendation for situations when the exchange rate is stable, and/or there is limited currency substitution. In the reverse case, it may be preferable to maintain required reserves on foreign currency deposits in foreign currency.

exceptions are Armenia, Azerbaijan, Belarus, and Kazakhstan, which allow the commercial banks to choose the currency in which to meet reserve requirements on foreign currency deposits.[7] While Azerbaijan, Belarus, Georgia, Russia, Tajikistan, Turkmenistan, and Uzbekistan keep reserve balances blocked throughout the compliance period, the rest of the countries have adopted reserve averaging.[8] Only Belarus, Estonia, the Kyrgyz Republic, and Moldova remunerate required reserves.[9]

Overdraft facilities that provide uncollateralized short-term credits at penalty rates are in place in Azerbaijan, Belarus, Russia, and Tajikistan.[10] In Turkmenistan, the central bank has introduced an auxiliary credit facility that provides banks with short-term credits. The rate is determined at a margin over the refinance rate to limit recourse to this facility.

Many countries—Armenia, Georgia, Kazakhstan, Kyrgyz Republic, Latvia, Moldova, and Ukraine—have moved toward the adoption of collateralized standing facilities (e.g., a Lombard window) to reduce the central bank's credit risk, as the stock of usable collateral (usually treasury bills) has increased. Lending through this facility is short term at a penalty rate. Russia has introduced a repo facility to allow primary dealers on the securities market to settle transactions. Azerbaijan established a rediscount mechanism in 1997, which allows banks to sell government securities to the central bank at a discount in an emergency. In Armenia, the central bank provides extended, uncollateralized "systemic" credit for up to one year. Countries with a currency board—Estonia and Lithuania—provide extensions of central bank credit to commercial banks within the limits imposed by the amount of foreign exchange reserves in excess of those needed to provide full backing of base money.

Credit auctions were introduced in most of the countries as a first step toward market-based monetary instruments and have been used at some time in all countries except those with a currency board—Estonia and, since 1995, Lithuania. Tajikistan introduced auctions in December 1997, and has carried out several since then. As the volume of treasury bills and government securities in the market has risen, the rate of collateralization required for credit received in the credit auction has increased, grad-

[7]In Armenia, since August 1997 at least 50 percent of reserve requirements on foreign currency deposits has to be met in foreign currency.

[8]In Georgia reserves are not averaged, as reserve balances (up to 90 percent) may be used as collateral for credit auctions. In Russia there is a very restrictive reserve averaging regime, and banks do not use this facility.

[9]Only excess reserves are remunerated in Estonia.

[10]Effective June 1998, uncollateralized short-term credits are no longer issued in Russia.

ually transforming the uncollateralized credit auctions into the equivalent of repurchase agreements. This phenomenon has occurred in Armenia, Latvia, Lithuania, Russia, and Ukraine. In addition, most countries have broadened the range of admissible collateral beyond treasury bills to include foreign exchange holdings, promissory notes, and some less liquid assets. Because of these developments, credit auctions are being phased out and are currently used actively only in Moldova, Tajikistan, and Uzbekistan. Credit auctions have been replaced by repo auctions in Latvia, and were recently suspended in the Kyrgyz Republic. In Moldova, the credit auction was expected to be fully replaced by open market operations by the end of 1998. In Turkmenistan, the auction was recently discontinued to avoid excessive liquidity expansion. In Russia, until mid-1996, low interbank market rates reduced interest in the credit auctions. The lower interbank rates were largely a reflection of stronger demand from regional markets outside Moscow. Auctions have not been frequent in Belarus, owing to the authorities' emphasis on directed credits. In Azerbaijan, recent improvements in regulation and information dissemination may foster the development of credit auctions.

Inflation, Financial Deepening, and Dollarization

Monetary programming has been hampered by unstable relationships between monetary aggregates and economic activity (this stems from sharp changes in money velocity) and inaccuracies in measurements of domestic product on which quantitative projections of money demand are based. Medium-term targets for inflation, for example, may be difficult to achieve simply because they are based on projections of the growth in monetary aggregates, which may be subject to wide fluctuations in velocity. Only recent data, usually comprising no more than three years, provide meaningful information, since the earliest observations displayed fluctuations that were largely caused by the one-time effect of the price liberalization shocks beginning in 1992. In addition, in most of the economies high inflation and a lack of confidence in the banking sector have induced a flight from the domestic currency (reflected in a large share of bank deposits held in foreign currencies) and a marked preference for liquidity (reflected in the relative importance of cash holdings in the broad money aggregate). Despite the difficulties in implementing a monetary program, some reference monetary program is needed in each of the countries under review. With the passage of time, the economies will achieve greater stability in monetary relationships, and the monetary authorities' ability to implement sound policies based on these data will be enhanced. Of course, those countries imple-

Figure 2.1. Real Broad Money
(Deflated by CPI; 1995 = 100)

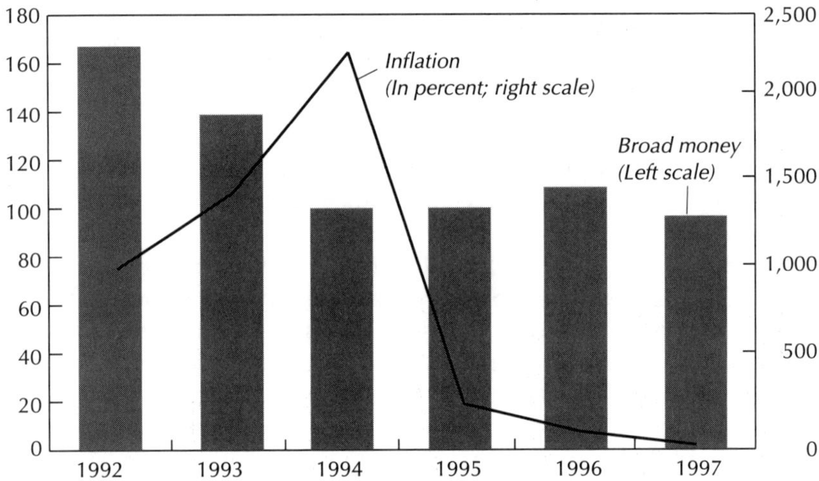

Sources: IMF staff estimates; and IMF, *World Economic Outlook.*
Note: Simple average of 15 countries. 1997 data are preliminary.

menting a fixed exchange rate regime cannot follow an independent monetary policy. In fact, the more the exchange rate is fixed, the less the scope for an independent monetary policy. Monetary operations will be geared toward preserving the exchange rate parity and therefore will reflect conditions in the market of the peg currency, with a risk differential.

Developments in Monetary Aggregates

The economies of the 15 countries in this study seem to have gone through at least two clearly identifiable stages. At the beginning of the transition, a combination of limited supply and government controls kept prices arbitrarily low and resulted in a significant accumulation of currency holdings and bank deposits (mostly demand). This phenomenon, often referred to as "monetary overhang," fueled high inflation rates at the time of the elimination of price controls. As prices skyrocketed, the real value of monetary aggregates fell significantly (Figure 2.1). With varying degrees of success, stabilization based on monetary restraint and tight fiscal policies rapidly brought inflation rates down to moderate levels. During this second phase, the real value of monetary aggregates stabilized, hovering around levels that were, on average, below those in

Figure 2.2. Inverse Velocity
(M2/GDP; in percent)

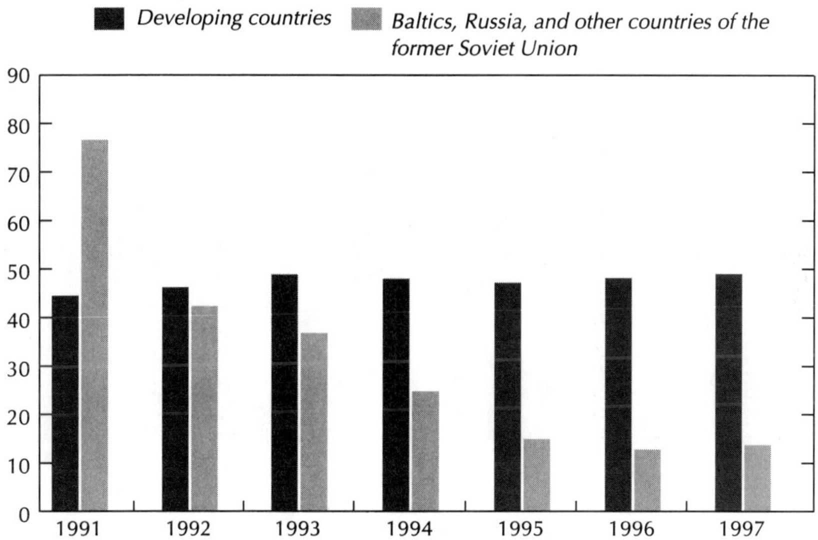

Sources: IMF staff estimates; and IMF, *World Economic Outlook*.
Note: Simple average of 15 countries. 1997 data are preliminary.

developing countries (Figures 2.2 and 2.3). Figure 2.4 shows a high and increasing share of the currency component in broad money, which is much higher in the Baltics, Russia, and other countries of the former Soviet Union than in other developing countries. This reflects in part the reactions of economic agents in those countries to the recent inflation spike, and attendant uncertainties, particularly with respect to the credit quality of banks, in the earlier stage of reform.

Money velocity has fluctuated significantly from 1991 through 1997, increasing substantially at the beginning of the reform, as the public reduced cash balances to minimize its exposure to price changes, a typical response to high and accelerating inflation. The public was reluctant to use the nascent banking sector, as indicated by a growing currency component of M3 (Figure 2.4), because of a lack of confidence in financial institutions, which was reinforced by several banking crises; a lack of familiarity with banking practices; and, in many cases, relatively low deposit rates, which stemmed from a paucity of profitable investment opportunities and excess liquidity. As Figure 2.5 shows, in most cases real deposit rates have turned positive only recently, albeit at low levels that have not induced a sizeable increase in bank deposits.

Figure 2.3. Inverse Velocity, 1997
(M2/GDP; in percent)

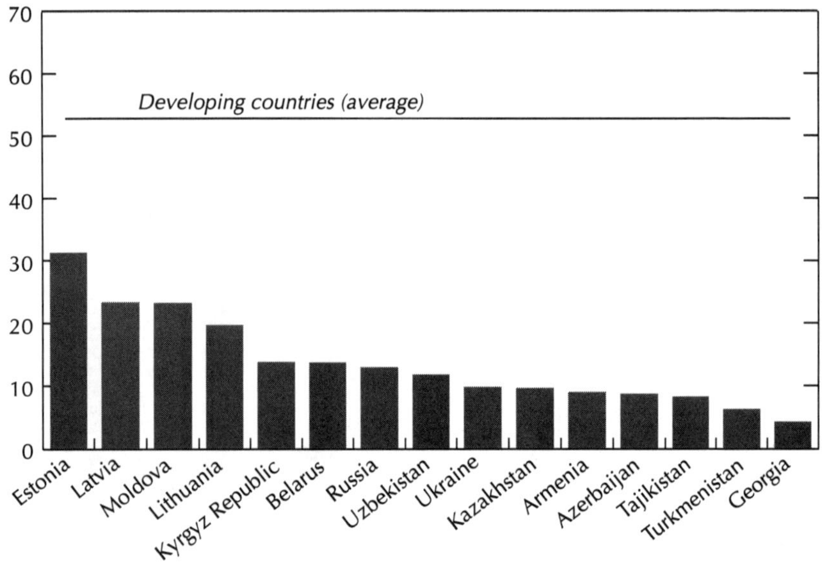

Sources: IMF staff estimates; and IMF, *World Economic Outlook*.
Note: Simple average of 15 countries. 1997 data are preliminary.

Dollarization

Dollarization presents both benefits and risks. For countries that have experienced extreme price instability and capital flight, dollarization has often played a key role in remonetization of the economy. But dollarization may also increase risks in the financial sector, including risks to foreign currency loan portfolios resulting from domestic currency devaluations, and to the ability of central banks to serve as lender-of-last-resort. Dollarized economies also have experienced losses in seignorage revenues.

Data on dollarization of deposits is at best fragmentary. There is no information on cross-border deposits, which are likely to have played an important part in the flight to quality during the first stages of the transition. Further caution is warranted when analyzing early developments, since changes in the dollar share of M3 may be in part explained by changes in the real exchange rate.[11]

[11]In practice, foreign currency holdings do not adjust continuously to changes in the macroeconomic environment. As a result, the currency composition of portfolios may fluctuate significantly in periods of sharp temporary movements in the real exchange rate, as the value of the stock of foreign currency assets vis-à-vis domestic currency assets changes accordingly.

Figure 2.4. Composition of M3
(In percent)

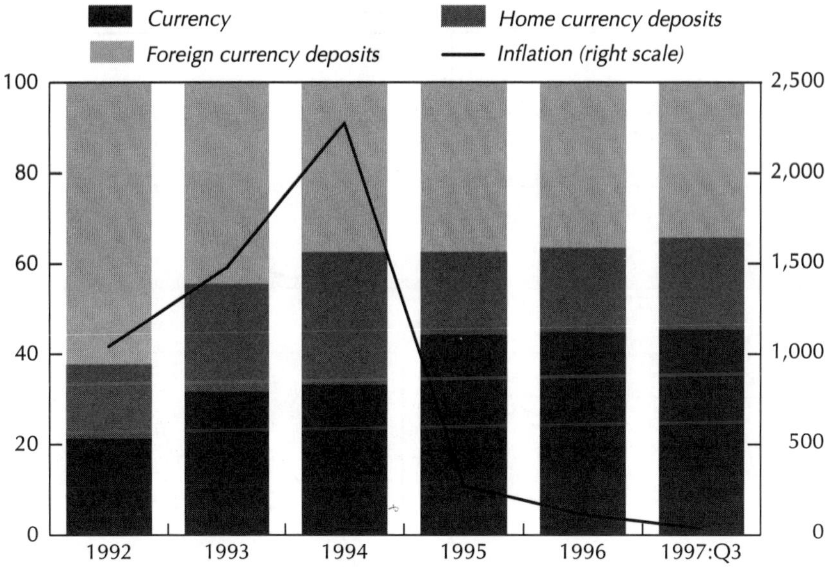

Sources: IMF staff estimates; and IMF, *World Economic Outlook.*
Note: Simple average of 15 countries.

Taking the above factors into account, the dollar plays a clear role in bank deposits in most of the 15 countries in this study, and its share of bank deposits has remained relatively stable as inflation has subsided and deposit rates have become positive in real terms (Figure 2.5).[12] On average, dollar deposits represent close to 40 percent of total deposits and, given the strong preference for liquidity, foreign currency holdings may also be substantial.[13]

Monetary Policy Indicators

Even in those countries where inflation has been contained and some of the basic ingredients for an effective monetary policy—central bank autonomy and active government securities and interbank markets—have

[12]In Estonia, household foreign currency deposits were allowed only in 1994.

[13]The standard measure of dollarization (dollar deposits over M3) is inappropriate, since it ignores cash foreign currency holdings while including in the denominator domestic currency holdings, which are relatively important in these countries. In many cases the structure of reserve requirements has to some extent favored dollar intermediation, by stipulating lower ratios on foreign currency deposits.

Figure 2.5. Real Deposit and Lending Rates

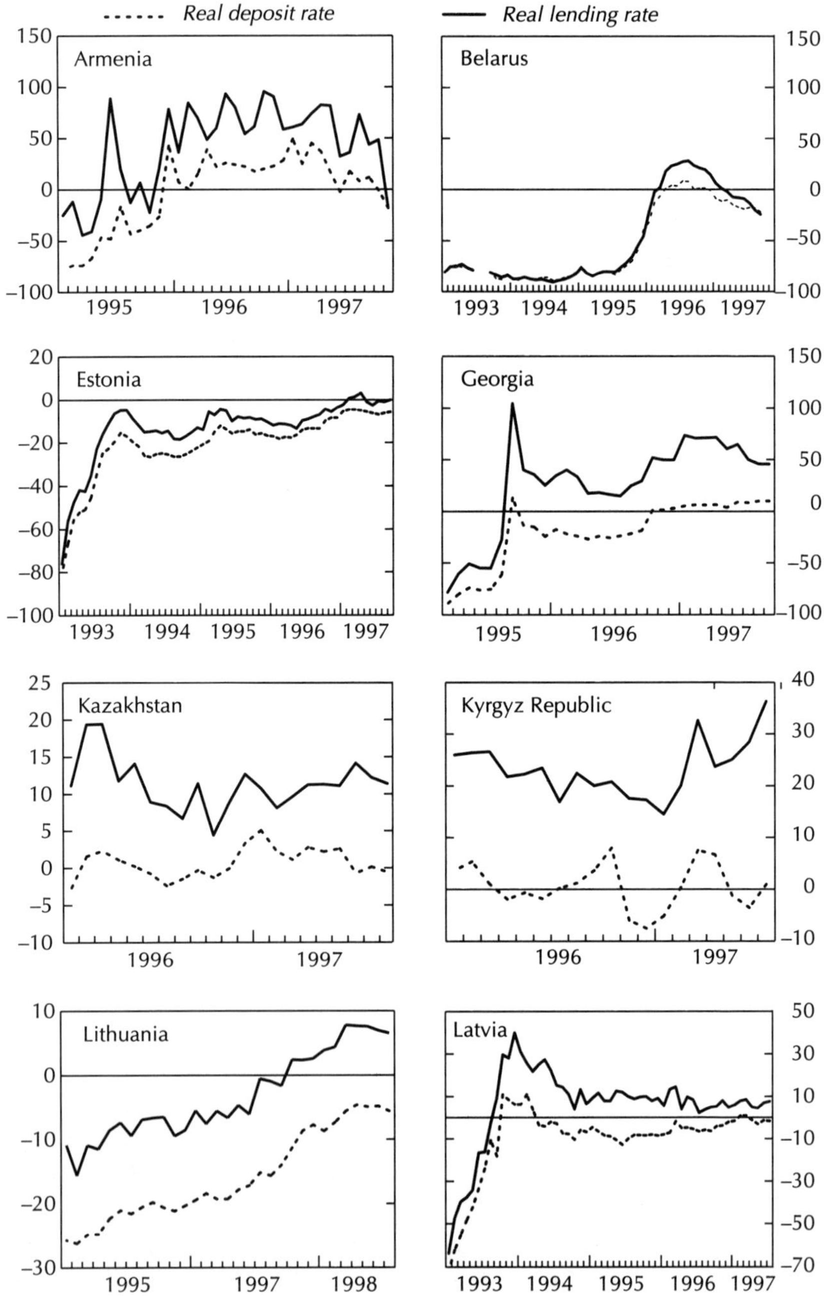

Figure 2.5 *(concluded)*

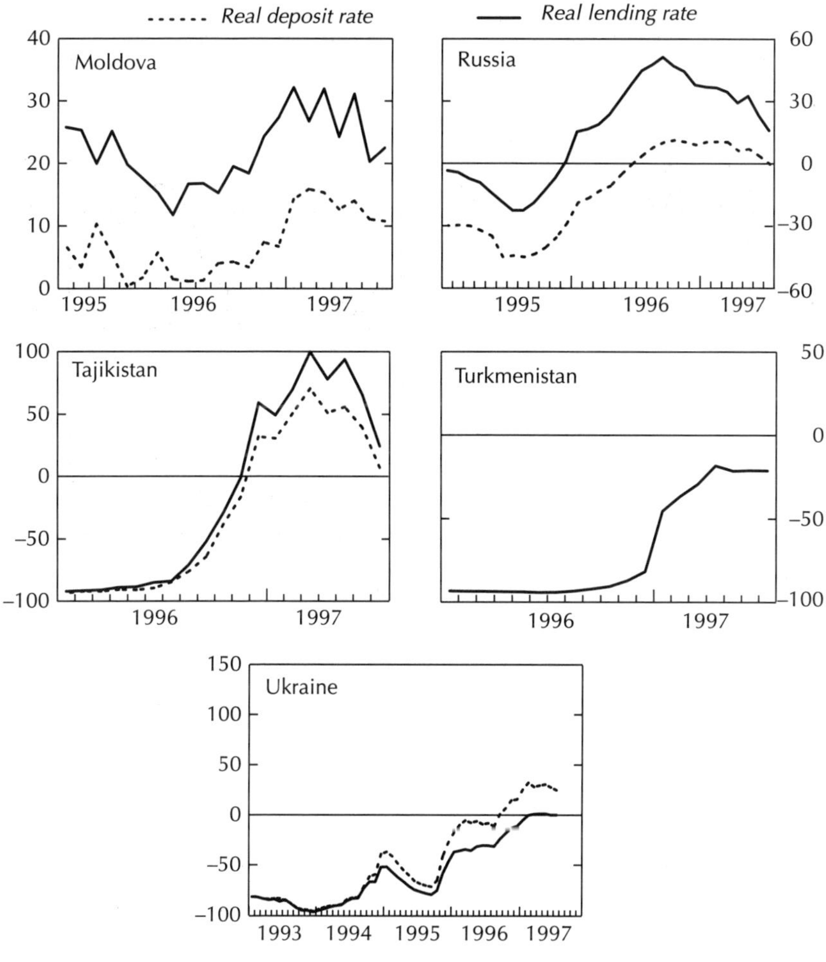

Source: IMF staff estimates.
Note: Real deposit rate data not available for Turkmenistan.

been put in place, much remains to be done in terms of liquidity forecasting and liquidity management. Figure 2.6 shows that reserve money displays significant volatility on a monthly basis, with average percentage changes ranging from around 4 percent in the Baltic countries to more than 10 percent in Tajikistan and Turkmenistan.

Although progress has been made in most countries (as shown by the declining path of the 12-month volatility of changes in reserve money), monthly fluctuations are still significant.

Figure 2.6. Reserve Money

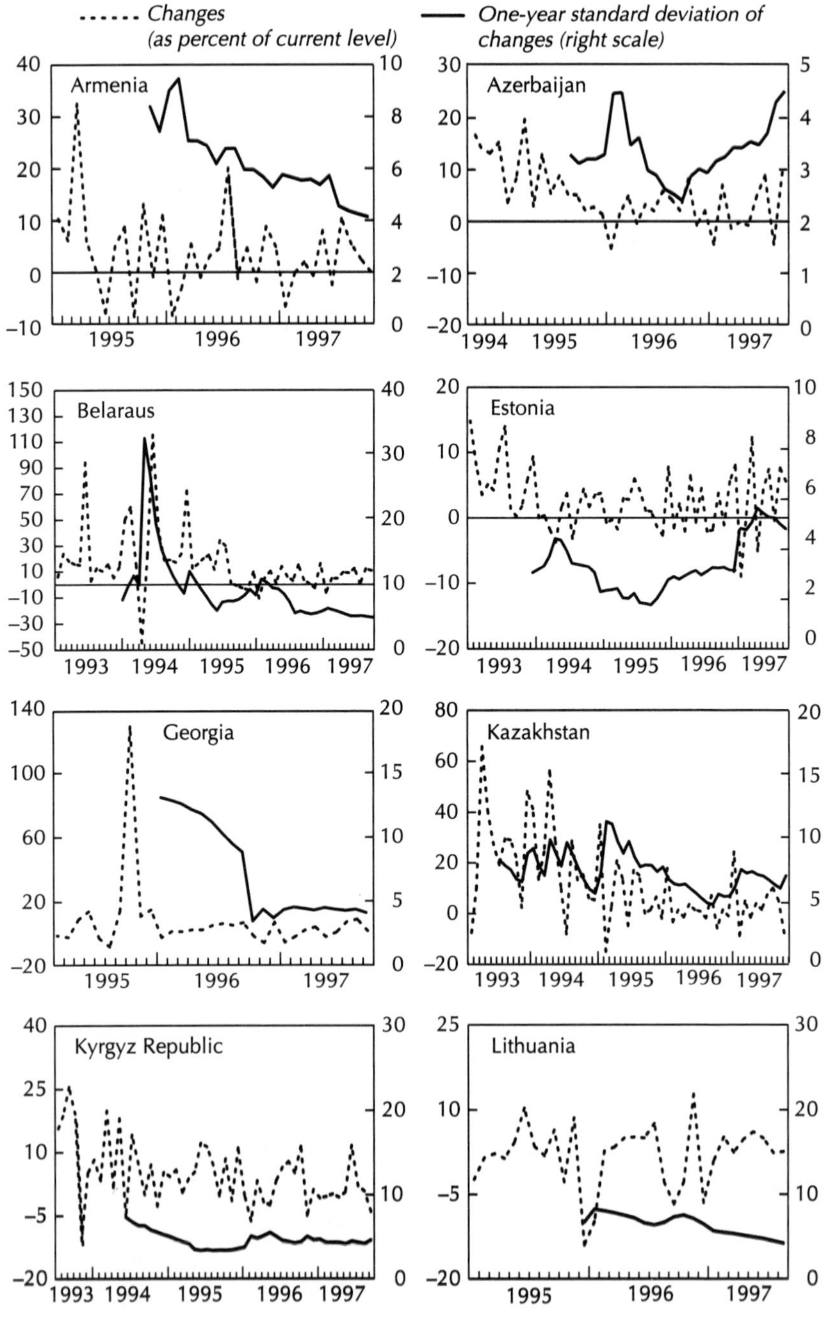

Figure 2.6 *(concluded)*

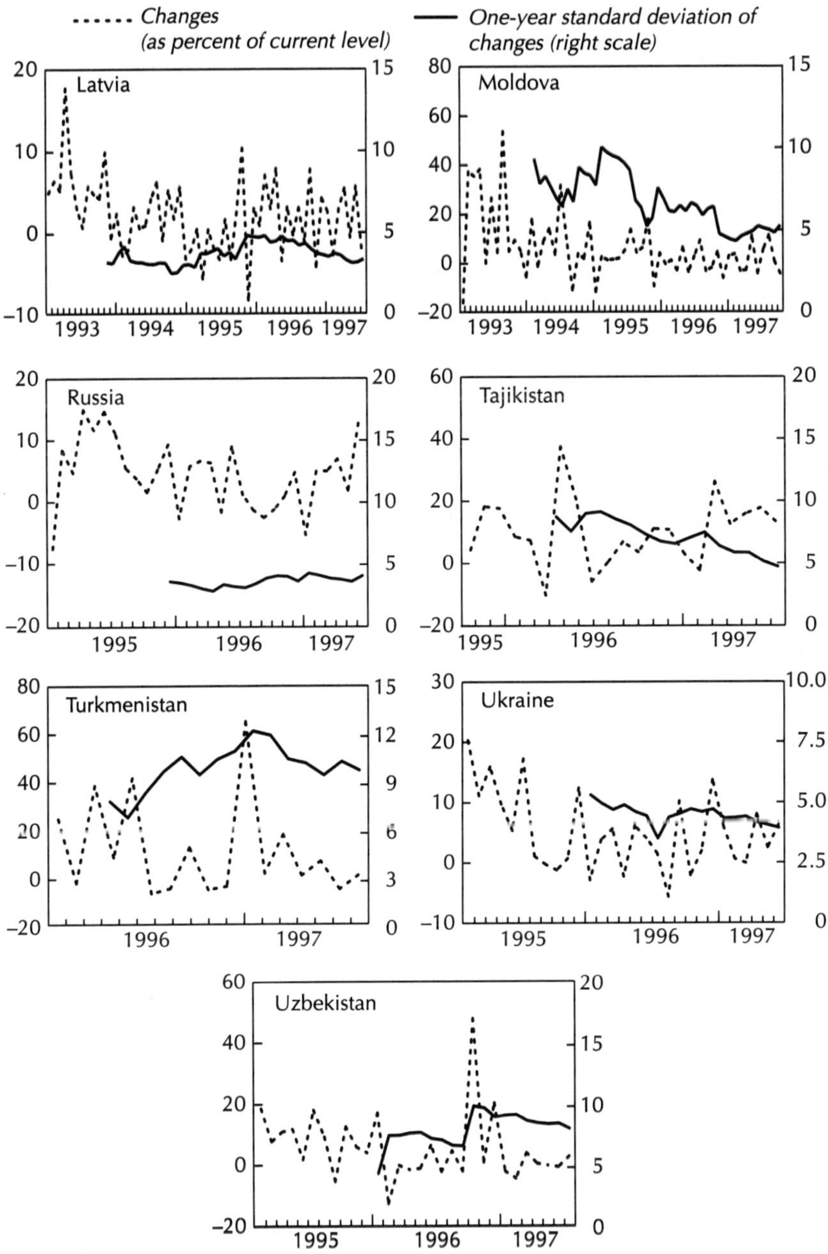

Source: IMF staff estimates.

More important, in most cases the link between reserve money and short-term market rates is weak or nonexistent, suggesting either that market participants do not engage in active liquidity management or that the interbank and securities markets are not yet developed to the point of actively reflecting changes in overall liquidity.[14] In either case, the transmission of monetary actions to market interest rates is likely to be highly inefficient, thus limiting the scope for an effective monetary policy.

An alternative that monetary authorities may use to influence interest rates is the direct management of a reference or refinance rate. This mechanism is particularly relevant to underdeveloped markets where the mechanism of price discovery is hampered by insufficient volume and a high degree of macroeconomic uncertainty, which in turn may yield highly volatile interest rates and deter participation in the absence of such a reference rate. Although a case-by-case analysis is necessary to assess the direction of causality, a cursory look at Figure 2.7 seems to support the hypothesis that, in most of the countries reviewed in this volume, short-term interest rates (deposit rate and three-month treasury bill) tend to follow the refinance rate set by the government.

Country Rankings

Table 2.1 presents country rankings that illustrate the relative development of monetary operations and government securities markets in the economies under review. Classification levels and criteria are the same as those used in previous background studies prepared for the Basle meetings.

The first criterion covers the quality of central bank facilities, that is, the mechanisms through which the central bank is able to manage liquidity at its own discretion, and the collateralized standing facilities that are available to banks to relieve liquidity shortages. A rating of "substantial" progress indicates that the central bank has: the ability to conduct operations in the secondary market for securities, either in the form of outright purchases and sales of securities, as in Kazakhstan, Russia, and Ukraine, or through repos and reverse repos, as in the Kyrgyz Republic, Latvia, Russia, and Ukraine; or a well-designed and functioning Lombard-type facility with well-specified rules of access (Kyrgyz Republic, Moldova, Russia, and Ukraine). "Moderate" progress implies that some or all of those facilities are in place, but they are subject to shortcomings, as in

[14]This may also be because in thin markets reported interest rates often reflect sporadic or diverse operations and transactions, including, for example, market transactions, or open market operations of different sizes or terms.

Figure 2.7. Interest Rates

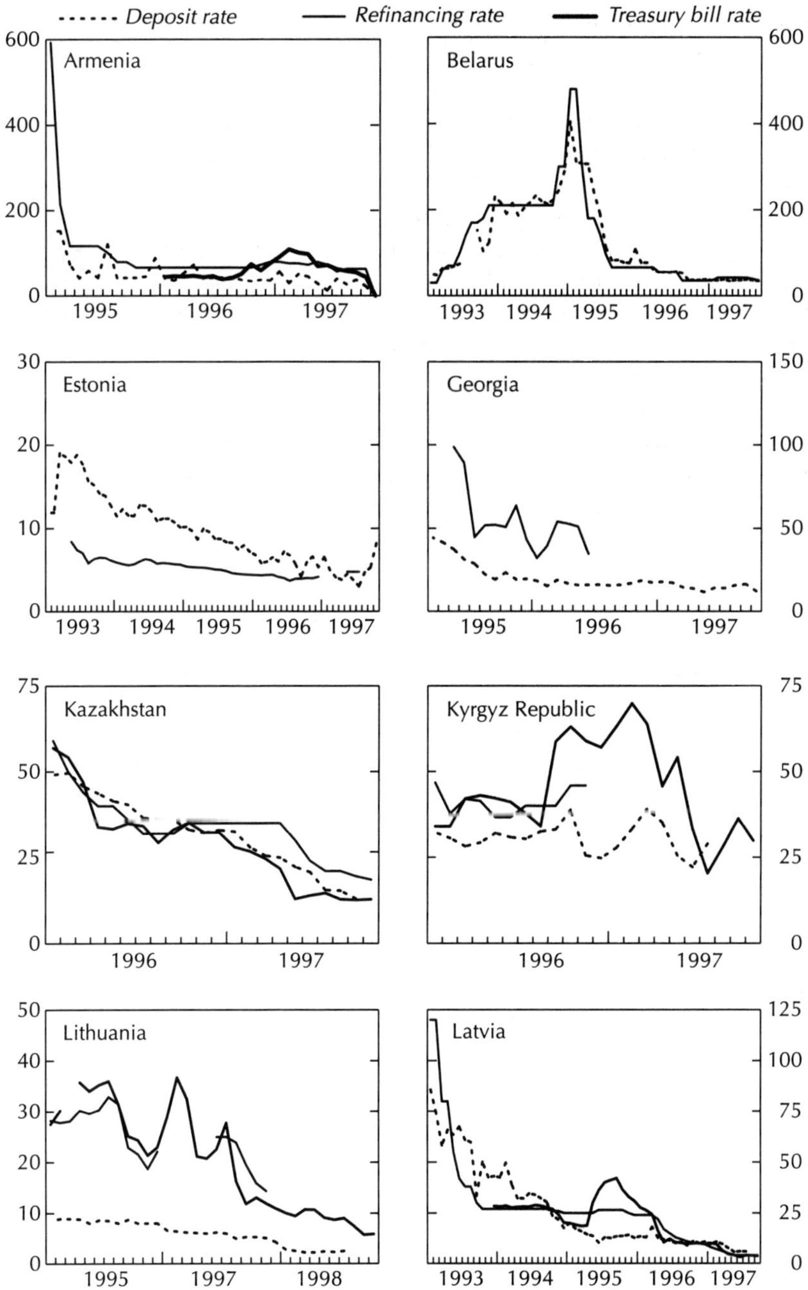

Figure 2.7 *(concluded)*

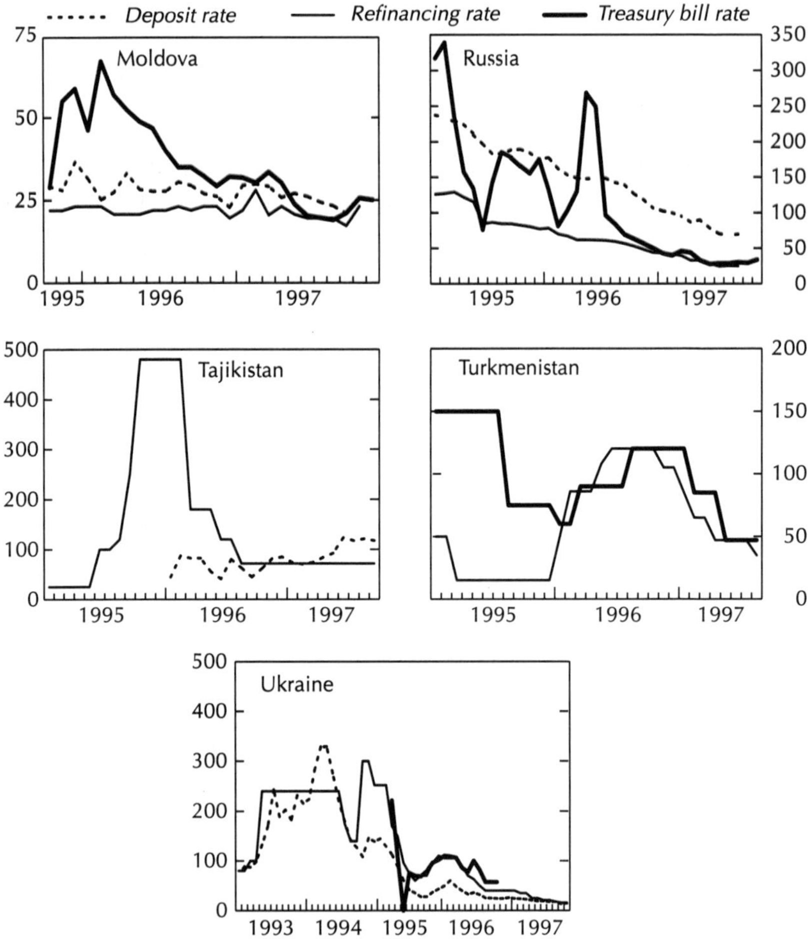

Source: IMF staff estimates.
Note: Treasury bill rate data not available for Belarus, Georgia, and Tajikistan.

Armenia, Georgia, and Uzbekistan. The remaining countries were assigned a "limited" progress rating (Azerbaijan, Belarus, Tajikistan, and Turkmenistan).[15]

[15]Estonia and Lithuania have currency board arrangements and thus do not actively manage banking system liquidity. Hence, they are excluded from this classification. In the second quarter of 1997, however, Lithuania issued rules on, and started to conduct, repo transactions to inject liquidity and deposit auctions to mop up liquidity, in anticipation of its forthcoming exit from the currency board arrangement.

The second criterion ranks banks on the basis of their operating framework for monetary policy implementation. Substantial progress implies that short-term monetary policy is based on the central bank's monetary program and short-term liquidity forecasts and that the bank uses monetary instruments consistent with its program, as in Kazakhstan, Kyrgyz Republic, and Russia. Where short-term coordination between the monetary program and the use of short-term indirect instruments was in place but could be strengthened, as in Armenia, Azerbaijan, Belarus, Georgia, Latvia, Moldova, and Ukraine, a moderate progress rating was assigned. The remaining countries—Tajikistan, Turkmenistan, and Uzbekistan—showed limited progress.

The third criterion evaluates the development of two markets: the interbank money market and the secondary market for government securities. Countries with active markets for interbank money and secondary exchanges of government securities—Kazakhstan, Latvia, and Russia—earned a substantial ranking. Those with an active market in one of the two areas—Georgia, Kyrgyz Republic, Moldova, Ukraine, and Uzbekistan—were ranked moderate. Countries with activity in neither type of market—Armenia, Azerbaijan, Belarus, Tajikistan, and Turkmenistan—were ranked limited.

Overall rankings were calculated as follows: substantial progress was given to countries that received substantial ratings in at least two categories. A rating of moderate progress required at least a moderate ranking in at least two of the three criteria. The remaining countries received limited ratings.

Priorities for Reform

Significant progress has been achieved since the initial stages of reform at the start of the decade, and most of the 15 countries under review have already put in place the basic ingredients conducive to an effective market-oriented monetary policy. But active liquidity management through indirect instruments within a short-term monetary policy framework, including full coordination between monetary and foreign exchange operations, still lies ahead for most of the central banks.[16] Although the underlying reasons are varied, all the countries must deal with the constraints imposed on liquidity forecasting and management by the lack of well-functioning interbank money markets and secondary markets for govern-

[16]Although open market operations are conducted on a frequent basis in many countries (Belarus, Kazakhstan, Kyrgyz Republic, Russia, Ukraine, and Uzbekistan), there seems to be no case in which the central bank relies solely on open market operations to attain its target level of liquidity.

ment securities—two elements that are crucial for the development of indirect monetary control.

Several factors impede active trading in the existing interbank markets: (1) a seeming lack of trust among market participants, reinforced by several past episodes of bank distress and concerns about the health of the financial system, as in Kazakhstan, Kyrgyz Republic, Latvia, and Lithuania; (2) inadequate regulation and supervision of bank activities; and (3) insufficient dissemination of information. An additional impediment relates to the large and irregular injections of liquidity through the extension of directed credits in some countries. Naturally, the phasing out of directed credits will be critical to development of the interbank markets in those cases. In this context, the buildup of the stock of collateral is likely to be beneficial for reducing credit risk, as is already apparent in the Kyrgyz Republic and Moldova. Moreover, efficient interbank clearing and settlement systems and timely information on correspondent account balances can stimulate daily trading of banks' liquidity positions, as in Georgia and Russia. Finally, improving the supervisory capacity of the central bank can go a long way to contain credit risk, where market activity is hindered by concerns about the financial condition of individual banks (Armenia, Kazakhstan, Kyrgyz Republic, and Lithuania).

Another area for reform is that of the secondary markets for government securities. Except for a few countries—Belarus, Kazakhstan, and Russia—these markets are small or nonexistent.[17] Standardization of trading arrangements, elimination of distorting taxes, and better information dissemination and transparency of primary auction results can help foster secondary market activity. In the medium term, a comprehensive framework for public debt management, yet to emerge in many cases, may further stimulate secondary markets. Pending tasks include extending the maturity profile of debt, capturing household savings, and creating a system of primary dealers to help develop secondary markets. Enhanced supervision and enforcement of performance criteria for primary dealers, and the establishment of rigorous settlement procedures, including a rapid move toward a delivery-versus-payment settlement, can generate a safer environment and more liquid securities markets.

As the volume of collateral increases, central banks should be expected to move toward collateralization of auctioned credit as a first step in replacing this instrument by repurchase auctions. The same is true for central bank uncollateralized credit facilities, which should eventually be transformed into Lombard windows. Such reforms, beside protecting the quality of the central bank assets, generate demand and liquidity in the

[17]Government securities markets have not developed in Estonia or Latvia because the two governments have not issued domestic debt instruments owing to their strong fiscal positions.

underlying instrument. In the design of their facilities and open market operations, however, central banks must take care not to discourage the use of the interbank market as the first source of bank liquidity.

Yet another priority is the work that remains to be done regarding data collection and calibration of bank liquidity forecasts. Monitoring of banks' excess reserves and interest rate movements should be conducted on a frequent basis, with special emphasis on the quality of the data. The use of desegregated data series and error control techniques, and a close monitoring and forecasting of government payments and receipts, which in turn requires a tight coordination with the treasury, may improve the accuracy of short-term projections.

A final priority concerns the need for the central bank to have the necessary volume of liquid and fully marketable securities in its own portfolio to be able to conduct substantial sterilization operations in the open market—all of which should be coordinated with the public debt program.

3

Foreign Exchange Markets and Official International Reserve Management

Bernard Laurens

As a group, the Baltics, Russia, and other countries of the former Soviet Union have achieved substantial progress in the areas of convertibility, foreign exchange market development, and central bank foreign exchange operations over the last six years. The institutional arrangement for an efficient market-based allocation of foreign exchange is in place in most countries; payments and transfers for current account transactions are free of restrictions, except in a limited number of countries; and several countries maintain a liberal system for capital account transactions, or interpret liberally the restrictions in place. Nominal exchange rates have begun to stabilize in most countries (Figure 3.1). The ratio of gross international reserves to imports also indicates that countries are moving to macroeconomic stabilization (Table 3.1). Foreign exchange markets are usually shallow, however, with banking unsoundness often an obstacle to market deepening.

Recent Developments

Out of the group, only four countries—Belarus, Tajikistan, Turkmenistan, and Uzbekistan—had not yet achieved current account convertibility (see Chapter 8, Table 8.4) by the end of 1997. During the past year, Armenia acceded to Article VIII of the IMF's Articles of Agreement, and Russia and Ukraine removed remaining restrictions on current account transactions.[1]

[1]Article VIII, Sections 2, 3, and 4 define the obligations of convertibility that IMF members are required to undertake. Under Section 2 members may not, without approval of the IMF, impose restrictions on the making of payments and transfers for current international transactions; under Section 3, members may not engage in discriminatory currency

Figure 3.1. Nominal and Real Effective Exchange Rates

(Indexed to 1980)

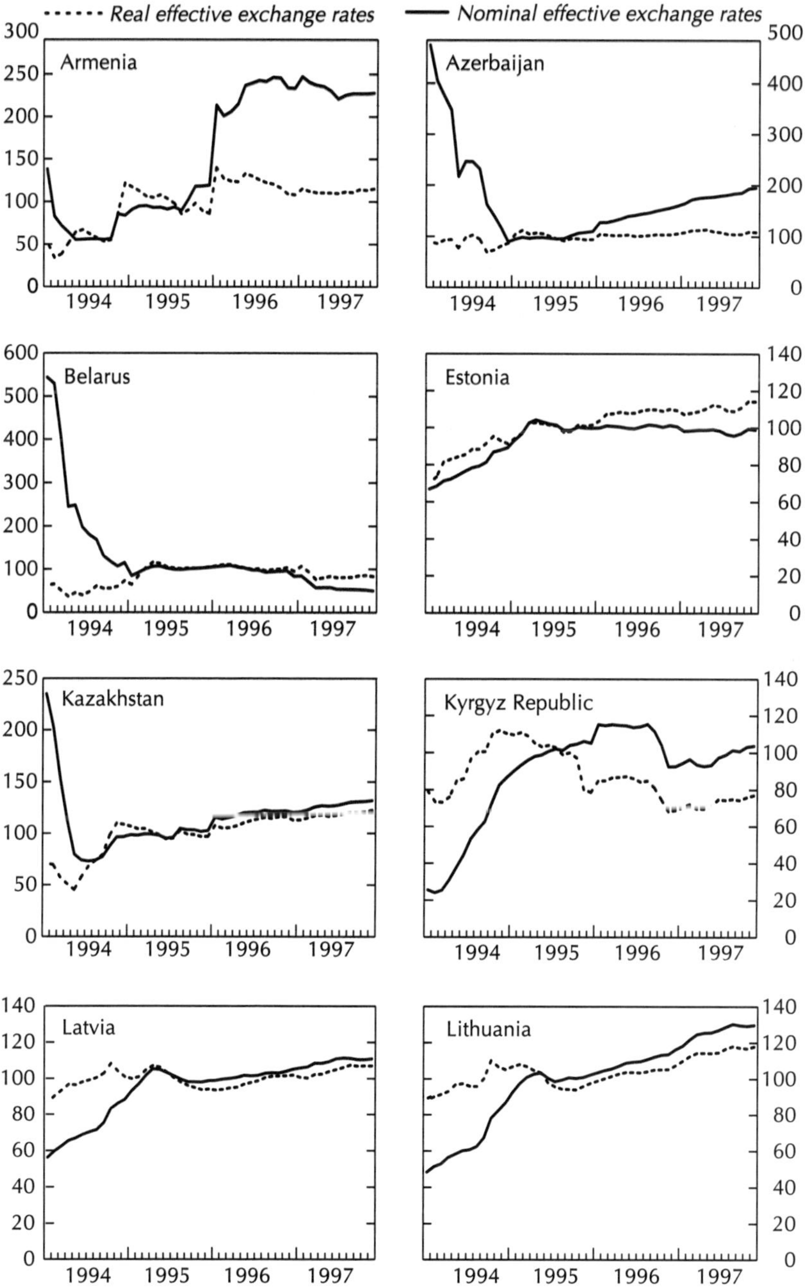

Figure 3.1 ***(concluded)***

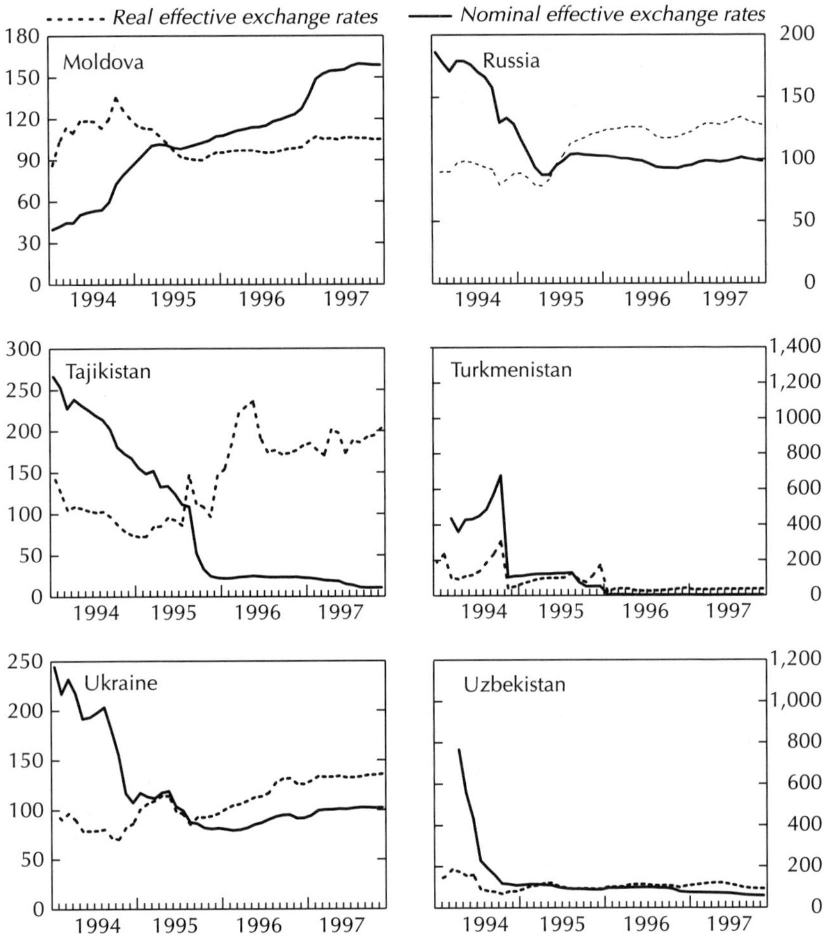

Source: IMF staff estimates.

Belarus, Turkmenistan, and Uzbekistan maintain a multiple-currency practice (subject to the jurisdiction of the IMF). Azerbaijan has virtually eliminated all restrictions, and plans to accede to Article VIII. In

arrangements or in multiple currency practices that are not approved by the IMF. Section 4 contains provisions regarding the convertibility of foreign-held balances. Russia eliminated one exchange restriction resulting from the inconvertibility of interest income on foreign holdings of government securities on January 1, 1998. In May 1997, Ukraine removed the last two remaining restrictions on payments and transfers for current account transactions.

Table 3.1. Ratio of Total Reserves to Imports
(In months)

	1992	1993	1994	1995	1996	1997[1]
Armenia	. . .	0.3	0.7	1.7	2.2	3.1
Azerbaijan	. . .	. . .	. . .	1.3	2	3.8
Belarus	. . .	0.3	0.3	0.7	0.6	0.5
Estonia	30.1	4.9	3.2	2.7	2.5	1.9
Georgia	. . .	. . .	0.7	2.7	2.7	2.5
Kazakhstan	0.4	1.6	3.5	3.7	3.1	3.2
Kyrgyz Republic	. . .	0.8	1.3	2.3	1.7	3.3
Latvia	0.7	4.4	4.6	3	3.1	3
Lithuania	0.5	1.9	2.5	2.5	2	2.9
Moldova	. . .	1.5	3.2	3.9	3.6	3.9
Russia	0.6	1.3	1.2	2.5	2	2.4
Tajikistan	. . .	. . .	. . .	0.1	0.3	0.2
Turkmenistan	11.2	6	7	9	9	16
Ukraine	0.8	0.1	0.5	0.8	1.1	1.4
Uzbekistan	0.6	3.8	5.9	6.2	4.8	3.5

Source: IMF staff estimates.
[1]Preliminary.

Tajikistan, political instability in late 1996 and early 1997 led to a disruption of foreign exchange reform and resulted in the reintroduction of import and export duties and of administrative mechanisms for allocating foreign exchange. The peace agreement in June 1997 allowed the authorities to eliminate all of the reintroduced restrictions. While most of the countries continued to require the repatriation of current account proceeds to domestic commercial banks (except for Armenia, Azerbaijan, the Baltics, and the Kyrgyz Republic), much progress was made in reducing or eliminating surrender requirements. In 1997, Belarus and Turkmenistan reduced, and Ukraine eliminated, surrender requirements.

Concerning capital account transactions, the Baltics, Georgia, and the Kyrgyz Republic had abolished controls on capital transactions prior to 1997, while Kazakhstan, Moldova, and Russia maintained limited controls. Only moderate progress was made in other countries during 1997, although Ukraine lifted the conditions for residents to borrow in foreign exchange from nonresidents.

Most of the countries have a unified exchange rate, except for Belarus and Uzbekistan, where different exchange rates still apply to different transactions, and those that maintain multiple-currency practices as mentioned above. Moreover, in some countries attempts to maintain overvalued official exchange rates and to restrict access to foreign exchange have caused cash/noncash spreads to rise substantially and have induced parallel exchange market activities in general with substantial spreads between official and parallel market rates.[2] The introduction of market-determined exchange rates, supported by monetary and fiscal discipline, eliminated the spread between these two markets in the other countries.

In the move toward market-oriented and liberal exchange systems, the market structures for foreign exchange trading have been organized as both interbank and auction-type arrangements, depending on the initial institutional circumstances. Although most countries under review made the development of an interbank foreign exchange market a priority, actually building a functional market has generally proved to be a challenging task.[3] Auction mechanisms were implemented at the start of the reform process, but they are gradually being phased out.[4] In a number of cases the auctions took the form of interbank exchanges and were a voluntary part of the overall exchange system. Establishing interbank foreign exchange markets is a priority because these markets allow a more decentralized allocation of foreign exchange than auctions. At the same time, interbank markets support a variety of exchange rate regimes, as indeed is the case in the countries represented, including both fixed and freely floating exchange rate regimes. The three Baltic countries formally peg their currencies (Estonia to the deutsche mark and Lithuania to the U.S. dollar through currency board arrangements; and Latvia to the SDR). Five others, including Russia and Ukraine, which both use exchange rate bands, and Georgia, Tajikistan, and Turkmenistan, de facto peg their exchange rates. The remaining seven countries operate regimes with varying degrees of flexibility—from allowing the interbank market to determine the exchange rate with negligible official intervention to having the central bank be the market-maker and set the rate.

The soundness of the banking system has been a key determinant of the development of interbank trading. This is evidenced in particular by the experience of Georgia, where the turnover on the interbank market represents 16 percent of total foreign exchange transactions on an aggregate basis, but reaches 50 percent for banks with good financial standing. Interbank trading has become relatively deep and competitive in the Baltic countries, Armenia, Georgia, Kazakhstan, the Kyrgyz Republic, Moldova, Russia, and Ukraine.[5]

[2]By the end of 1997, in Tajikistan the spread was brought down to about 13 percent while it reached about 30 percent in Belarus and Turkmenistan and about 110 percent in Uzbekistan.

[3]Azerbaijan was the last country to lift the prohibition on interbank trading (August 1997).

[4]The change in the auction format in the Kyrgyz Republic in February 1997 gave rise to a multiple-currency practice, which the IMF's Executive Board approved until December 1998.

[5]The share of interbank trading in total foreign exchange transactions has grown to 65 percent in Kazakhstan, 39 percent in the Kyrgyz Republic, 98 percent in Moldova, and to more than 80 percent in Russia.

In parallel with the development of interbank foreign exchange markets, there has been a general trend toward a shift of foreign exchange interventions by central banks from auction arrangements to interbank trading. This trend was reinforced in 1997 when the Central Bank of Armenia discontinued its interventions at the auction. Other countries in which the central bank intervenes exclusively in the interbank market include Latvia and Ukraine. The central bank continues to intervene exclusively at the auction in Belarus, Georgia, the Kyrgyz Republic, Tajikistan, Turkmenistan, and Uzbekistan. These dissimilarities in central banks' operating procedures reflect to a large extent the level of development of the countries' foreign exchange interbank markets, or, as in the Kyrgyz Republic, the need to channel donor funds to the market.

In most of the countries, central banks have attained an adequate organization of their foreign exchange departments, including achieving the separation of front and back offices (except in Azerbaijan, Tajikistan, and Uzbekistan), the adoption of settlement procedures in line with international standards and adequate reporting and accounting standards, and the use of suitable equipment. Refinements may be needed in some cases, however—for example, better reporting and coordination between front and back offices, and more back-office training, as is needed in the Kyrgyz Republic.

Most of the countries have also made significant progress in centralizing foreign exchange reserves at the central bank and in managing these reserves. A small portion of Russia's official reserves, however, is still held by the Ministry of Finance and by former Soviet trade banks. Presidential control over the country's official reserves continues in Turkmenistan; and in Uzbekistan the state-owned National Bank of Economic Activity administers a significant portion of the official reserves. In addition, some official reserves of Belarus are still held in domestic banks.

In the Baltics, the Kyrgyz Republic, Moldova, Russia, and Ukraine, foreign exchange reserve management has been relatively advanced for some time. Substantial progress has been made recently in developing adequate guidelines in a number of countries, including Armenia, Azerbaijan, Belarus, Georgia, Kazakhstan, and Turkmenistan. Further work is needed in Tajikistan and Uzbekistan to introduce meaningful guidelines and reporting procedures.

Country Rankings

Based on the level of development that has been achieved since the beginning of reforms, Table 3.2 groups countries into three categories. Countries in Group III (the Baltics, Armenia, Georgia, Kazakhstan, Kyrgyz Republic, Moldova, Russia, and Ukraine) have made substantial

Table 3.2. Country Rankings in Foreign Exchange Operations and Markets and in Official International Reserve Management

I Limited Progress	II Moderate Progress	III Substantial Progress	
Belarus	Azerbaijan	Armenia	Latvia
Tajikistan		Estonia	Lithuania
Turkmenistan		Georgia	Moldova
Uzbekistan		Kazakhstan	Russia
		Kyrgyz Republic	Ukraine

progress in most or all areas of foreign exchange reform. Ukraine has joined this group through the notable progress made in 1997. There is now only limited need for further reforms in this group, although specialized advice may still be needed in several of these countries to refine interbank market development, international reserve management policies, and coordination with monetary policy. Azerbaijan, the only country in the moderate category, has also shown reasonable progress, although the need for further reforms continues in a number of broad areas, including reserve management policies. Foreign exchange reforms in Group I—Belarus, Tajikistan, Turkmenistan, and Uzbekistan—have been slow, or have even been reversed. Slow progress in implementing structural and economic reforms and limitations in implementation capacity (Tajikistan and Turkmenistan) appear to be major impediments to progress. Likewise, a cautious approach to adopting market-oriented reforms, and even a lack of conviction as to the merits of such reforms constitutes an important impediment in Turkmenistan and Uzbekistan.

Priorities for Future Reform

Most of the countries of the Baltics, Russia, and the other countries of the former Soviet Union have implemented the key reforms required for an efficient market-based allocation of foreign exchange. Countries lagging behind are those that either did not consider such an approach to be appropriate given the country's specific circumstances, or that, in the wake of political instability, could not implement the necessary reforms. For these countries, one of the first priorities will be to implement the necessary measures for the acceptance of IMF's Article VIII.

In some of the countries, interbank foreign exchange markets have not yet begun. Others face the challenge of further enhancing market liquidity and depth so that the interbank market becomes the main channel for allocating foreign exchange. In both cases, central banks must intervene in a way that provides incentives for participants to start trading among themselves. This intervention can occur by trading through either an interbank exchange (i.e., a two-sided auction and with the market as a whole), or selected and reliable banks. Central bank intervention should evolve in phase with market development. Transitional arrangements, such as an interbank exchange, may well be used in tandem with over-the-counter interbank trading, depending on a country's circumstances and its objectives, and until the interbank market has reached a level of development that will allow reliance on interbank trading.

The pace for phasing out auction mechanisms and relying exclusively on interbank trading will depend on the circumstances of individual countries, and in particular on the stability of foreign exchange flows, the liquidity and solvency of some banks, the degree of trust between dealers, and the effectiveness of payment and communication systems. Progress in two areas appears to be critical: first, enhancing the soundness of the banking system so that banks are willing to trade with each other; and, second, eliminating surrender requirements. Technical refinements are also called for, including tightening or strengthening the enforcement of open position limits, improving settlement systems and correspondent relations, training dealers, and establishing codes of conduct.

As a consequence of macroeconomic stabilization and the return of investor confidence, a number of countries benefited from sustained capital inflows during much of 1997 (Armenia, Kazakhstan, Kyrgyz Republic, Moldova, Russia, and Ukraine). Large and volatile capital flows call for effective coordination between money and foreign exchange operations, as well as for the development of strategies for a smooth transition between alternative monetary and exchange arrangements. This is an area in which well-targeted technical assistance may be required in the near future. Some countries (Ukraine most recently), however, experienced sudden reversals of capital inflows. Such a situation calls for the design of contingency strategies to deal with such reversals.

Finally, the most advanced countries that have not yet fully liberalized capital account transactions—Kazakhstan, Moldova, Russia, and Ukraine—need to develop a strategy for an orderly liberalization of these transactions, consistent with macroeconomic stabilization and financial system reform. Achieving this kind of strategy may also call for well-targeted technical assistance. In Chapter 8, Table 8.5 provides details on where further work is needed in individual countries.

4

Banking Sector Reform

Claudia Dziobek and Jan Willem van der Vossen

The perestroika policies of the Soviet Union during the late 1980s set the stage for the rapid rise in the number of banks in individual states, although the ratio of credit to GDP remained low (see Chapter 8, Table 8.7). Concurrently, lax licensing policies and implementation of licensing requirements allowed many unsuitable banks to remain in the system in the early 1990s. At the same time, significant macroeconomic imbalances created conditions that gave banks incentives to engage in high-risk activities, such as foreign currency speculation. Weak banking laws and enforcement mechanisms failed to contain speculation by banks and to enforce safe and sound banking practices. As macroeconomic stabilization took hold, inflation declined and exchange rates stabilized. Banking problems of a systemic nature began to appear in the majority of countries because profits from speculation plummeted. Resulting bank insolvencies, sometimes entailing significant losses to depositors, damaged public confidence. But the countries have undertaken efforts to develop systemwide policies that address these issues and to restore bank soundness and the public confidence necessary to mobilize savings more effectively.

Underdeveloped legal, accounting, and judicial infrastructures also contributed to the slow development of traditional banking business (i.e., commercial, housing, and consumer lending). In the absence of effective legislation on loan contracts and collateral, reliable financial information on borrowers, and weak enforcement of credit contracts, lending remained a high-risk, low-return business. Moreover, the abundant issuance of government securities, mirroring high fiscal deficits, provided safe, high-yield alternative investments for banks.

With bank assets at an estimated cross-country average of 35 percent of GDP in 1997 (Figure 4.1), most national banking sectors in the countries in this study have not reached the level needed to adequately support eco-

Figure 4.1. Total Banking Assets, 1995–97
(In percent of GDP)

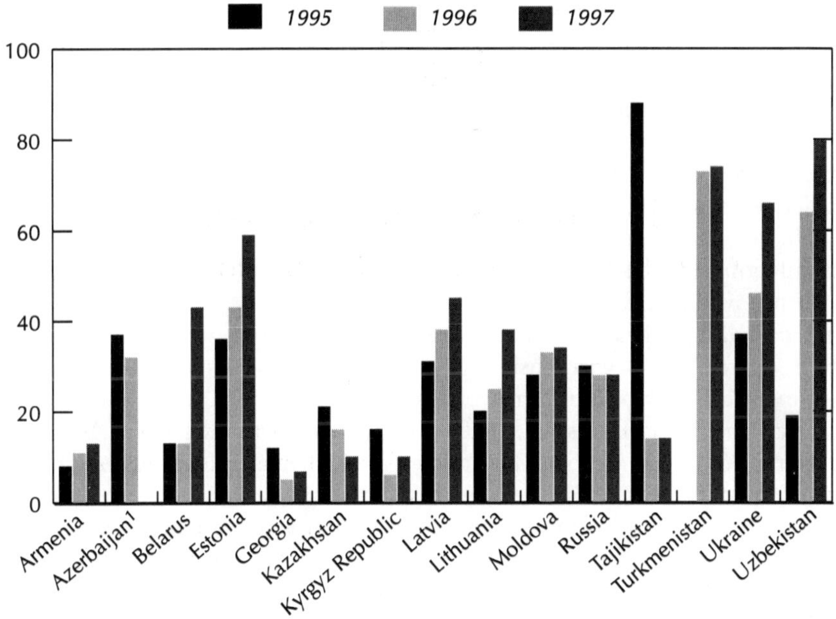

Source: Country authorities.
[1]1995 data not available; 1994 data used.

nomic growth.[1] In addition to the causes mentioned above, low intermediation has stemmed from high levels of barter, intercompany credit, arrears, and, in Russia, the widespread use of promissory notes. In essence, many banks have acted as investment funds, neglecting commercial lending, or as treasuries for other business interests of their shareholders. In nine of the countries under review, the proportion of total private sector loans to GDP is reported to have increased in 1997.[2] Even in these countries, however, levels are still very low, averaging some 12 percent of GDP.[3] In terms of the ratio of bank assets to GDP, financial intermediation has decreased in four of the countries.[4] Deposits relative to GDP have increased in nine of the countries, although absolute levels are still

[1]This simple average masks a wide dispersion ranging from 8 percent to 80 percent in the data for individual countries; the standard deviation of the statistic is about 26 percent.

[2]Armenia, Belarus, Estonia, Latvia, Lithuania, Moldova, Turkmenistan, Ukraine, and Uzbekistan.

[3]Some countries report much higher figures, but this may reflect different statistical methods.

[4]Kazakhstan, Kyrgyz Republic, Russia, and Tajikistan.

very low. With the exception of the state-guaranteed savings banks, which have generally attracted the bulk of household deposits, the new commercial banks have had very low levels of household deposits.

Important initiatives in banking sector reform have been taken by all countries, supported by much multilateral and bilateral technical cooperation. Most countries have tightened market-entry requirements, forced unfit banks to exit, and recapitalized or merged weak but viable banks, but the restructuring process is not yet complete.[5] Remaining insolvent and inactive banks will need to be closed, and many viable banks will need to undergo operational and financial restructuring. Although basic prudential regulations have been adopted in many key areas, implementation needs to be improved in specific areas, notably in loan classification, provisioning, and calculation of capital adequacy. Banking supervisory practices will need to be more incisive, with onsite inspection focused on asset quality and the payment capacity of the borrower. As countries gain experience with new supervisory frameworks, the need for further refinements will become apparent, and will need to be addressed. The final stages of building a sound banking system and effective supervision, tailored to local conditions, will need to be the primary responsibility of the countries themselves. A key area for improvement is the introduction of internationally accepted accounting standards and prudential reporting systems, without which good bank management and effective supervision are not possible.

As economic growth resumes in many of the 15 countries and the demand for credit and financial services increases, the following two years will be crucial for the development of the banking systems. The bank restructuring process should be vigorously pursued, and a banking supervisory function that can prevent recurrence of banking sector problems should be firmly established.

Bank Restructuring

In the Baltics, Russia, and the other countries of the former Soviet Union, the breadth of banking system problems has warranted some form of comprehensive restructuring strategy, starting with a broad diagnostic exercise (see Chapter 8, Table 8.8). Twelve countries have conducted such system-wide diagnostic reviews as a basis for a policy response.[6] Seven countries have formulated overall bank restructuring policies.[7] Other countries have taken a bank-by-bank approach. In eight countries, a central policy body has

[5]The Kyrgyz Republic, Lithuania, and Moldova report that a small number of banks remain in critical condition.

[6]All but Latvia, Lithuania, and Tajikistan.

[7]Belarus, Georgia, Kazakhstan, Kyrgyz Republic, Moldova, Russia, and Uzbekistan.

been created to deal with bank restructuring issues.[8] The majority of countries have not yet seen a compelling need to create an asset management agency, although the Kyrgyz Republic and Lithuania have done so.

Strategy and Institutional Framework

Beginning in 1996, the 15 countries began to implement a number of long-term strategies. First, they began to bolster bank licensing requirements, imposing higher capital requirements and reducing the number of new licenses issued. Second, they strengthened bank exit policies. During 1997, liquidations of insolvent institutions continued in Georgia, Kazakhstan, the Kyrgyz Republic, Lithuania, Moldova, Russia, and Ukraine. These measures have considerably decreased the number of banks, thus somewhat reducing the scope of the problem. Third, the 15 countries have continued to reinforce their overall banking supervision capacities, attempting to limit further deterioration of the banking system and to prevent a recurrence of problems. Fourth, a majority of countries have started to implement bank restructuring policies, including financial as well as operational restructuring, involving mergers and split-offs, restrictions on the activities of the weak banks in the system, and initial attempts to restructure the large formerly state-owned banks. In all cases, the countries under review indicated that in 1997 they were continuing these policies, which had proven to be effective. Particularly in the case of operational restructuring, these are not one-off measures, but efforts extending over several years.

In many of the countries, the authorities have received assistance in their restructuring programs from the IMF and the World Bank, as well as other agencies. World Bank Financial Sector Adjustment Loans or other instruments have explicitly addressed banking sector reform in Armenia, Azerbaijan, Estonia, Kazakhstan, the Kyrgyz Republic, Latvia, Lithuania, Moldova, and Uzbekistan. The IMF has collaborated closely with the World Bank in a number of the countries.[9]

Restructuring Policies

In the past two to three years, the mix of restructuring policies has varied across countries. Most countries reviewed in this study have mandat-

[8]Armenia, Azerbaijan, Kazakhstan, Kyrgyz Republic, Lithuania, Moldova, Russia, and Uzbekistan. A bank resolution unit was established within the National Bank of Ukraine to deal with problem banks.

[9]Under the agreed distribution of labor between the World Bank and the IMF, the World Bank has tended to focus on issues relating to individual banks, whereas the IMF has focused on overall banking sector soundness and the macroeconomic linkages between banking soundness and macroeconomic policy.

ed higher capital requirements for banks, in some cases through a phased approach extending several years—for example, Armenia, Azerbaijan, Georgia, and Russia. Countries have also introduced more stringent loan classification and provisioning rules for doubtful and past due loans. These measures have jointly forced banks to attract additional capital, merging or terminating their activities, a process that continued during 1997. Central banks have in certain cases injected additional liquidity into the system, in order to preserve stability in the short term, as in Armenia, Kazakhstan, Russia, and Ukraine in 1997. Judging whether such liquidity support constitutes short-term bridge financing rather than solvency support for unsound banks is often very difficult. In some cases impaired assets have been removed from banks' balance sheets and placed in asset management bodies. In other instances, supervisory authorities have imposed temporary administration upon troubled banks.

An important weakness in three countries—Moldova, Russia, and Ukraine—has been a reluctance to restructure the large banks, which control the bulk of the assets, with the result that efforts to date have focused on smaller banks. In some cases, large banks have lobbied against restructuring attempts. Nevertheless, the authorities will need to deal with large banks urgently, since they influence market confidence, and will need to be sufficiently healthy and well-managed to successfully process enhanced intermediation demands in the coming years. In Russia, systemically important banks are subject to intensive monitoring by a separate department within the central bank; these banks are also being separately monitored by a World Bank-led group of international bank supervisors.

Banking Sector Consolidation

In most of the countries the banking sector is undergoing a healthy process of consolidation as a result of firmer exit policies, tighter licensing policies, and, less frequently, more bank mergers (e.g., Kazakhstan). Overall, the total number of banks in the 15 countries decreased from more than 3,600 in 1994 to about 2,500 at the end of 1997 (Table 4.1). In Russia, which has the greatest concentration of banks, the number of banks has fallen from more than 2,500 at the end of 1994 to 1,764 at the end of 1997. In the Baltic countries, the total number of banks has declined from 107 to 55. A substantial number of banks have also closed in Armenia, Azerbaijan, Georgia, and Kazakhstan. This trend has allowed the remaining banks to grow in size and to increase their capital levels.

Operational Restructuring

Operational restructuring measures have focused on enhancing the safety and soundness of commercial bank operations by imposing restrictions on new lending, forcing banks to follow more aggressive loan col-

Table 4.1. Number of Banks, by Country

Country	1994	1995	1996	1997
Armenia	52	35	33	30
Azerbaijan	211	180	136	102
Belarus	47	40	38	37
Estonia	23	18	14	12
Georgia	229	101	61	53
Kazakhstan	191	130	101	98
Kyrgyz Republic	18	18	18	20
Latvia	57	40	33	32
Lithuania	27	16	12	11
Moldova	26	27	21	22
Russia	2,517	2,295	2,030	1,764
Tajikistan	16	19	23	26
Turkmenistan	—	—	15	67[1]
Ukraine	226	230	228[2]	225[3]
Uzbekistan	26	18	29	29
Total	3,666	3,167	2,792	2,526

Source: Country authorities.
[1]Includes 52 branches of the former Agroprom Bank.
[2]188 active.
[3]189 active.

lection policies, imposing more adequate provisioning policies, and introducing regulations on banks' internal procedures, including better loan allocation policies. In some cases, operational restructuring has taken the form of mergers or split-offs, in which viable parts are separated from nonviable parts. In some countries, such as Russia, considerable efforts are being undertaken by the World Bank, European Bank for Reconstruction and Development (EBRD), and other international agencies to improve the operational capabilities of commercial banks. The World Bank's Financial Institutions Development Program, launched in 1995 to improve commercial bank management, was given renewed attention in 1997. Twinning arrangements between foreign banks and domestic banks are being concluded; the EBRD has provided lines of credit and equity participation; and the European Union (EU) continues to provide consultancy services to banks in a number of countries.

The workout of nonperforming loans remains a problem that many countries—such as Moldova and Ukraine—place high on the agenda for future work. Some countries—Kyrgyz Republic, Latvia, and Ukraine—blame problems in the legal system for obstructing effective loan workout. Several countries—among them Estonia, Kazakhstan, and Kyrgyz Republic—stress the need for banks to develop better credit assessment skills to reduce losses in the future.

Financial Restructuring

Authorities in the countries under review have generally emphasized recapitalization by the institutions themselves and their shareholders, combined with operational restructuring techniques, and have generally refrained from suggesting government-funded financial rescue operations. In a number of countries, banks have been obliged to prepare recapitalization plans involving additional capital injections by shareholders and retention of dividends. In general, these countries have introduced policies to increase capital levels in all banks. In some cases, however, governments have contributed to the recapitalization of specific undercapitalized institutions, for instance state-owned banks. In eight countries the government has either made direct loans or directly assumed liabilities of ailing banks.[10] In addition, banks are under pressure to seek additional capital through increased minimum capital requirements, enhanced capital adequacy requirements, and higher provisions.

Country Rankings on Bank Restructuring

The 1997 assessment of progress in designing and implementing bank restructuring programs was broadly based on (1) completion of a diagnosis of problems in the banking system; (2) development of a restructuring strategy; and (3) creation of an institutional framework. The rankings in the 1998 survey are based on further progress in 1997 relative to 1996, as shown in the data provided by the countries and compiled in the tables, and supplemented by other sources (Table 4.2). The rankings provide only an approximation of progress made, since they are based on information that is uneven across countries, and on information from various sources, as well as subjective assessments. Countries were "upgraded" if substantial progress could be detected in at least one of the three areas of bank restructuring.

Banking Supervision

In general, good progress has been made in strengthening prudential regulations. Banks' adherence to these regulations, and in particular an appropriate assessment of loan quality, remains a problem, and rapid adoption of International Accounting Standards by commercial banks is essential for further progress.

[10]Azerbaijan, Belarus, Kazakhstan, Kyrgyz Republic, Latvia, Moldova, Turkmenistan, and Uzbekistan.

Table 4.2. Bank Restructuring

I Limited Progress	II Moderate Progress	III Substantial Progress
Belarus	Azerbaijan	Armenia
Tajikistan	Lithuania	Estonia
Turkmenistan	Russia	Georgia
	Ukraine	Kazakhstan
	Uzbekistan	Kyrgyz Republic
		Latvia
		Moldova

Prudential Regulations

In the majority of countries in this study, the minimum capital required to obtain a banking license has been raised to acceptable levels, with minimums set at the equivalent of $1 million, and, in many cases, at the EU standard of the equivalent of 5 million euro. This represents major progress compared to only a few years ago, when a bank could be opened with some tens of thousands of dollars. These policies have contributed to a decrease in the number of banks, and have helped ensure that new banks start business with the critical mass needed to establish reliable business operations and to serve as a cushion for start-up losses.

Capital adequacy levels are the principal indicators of banks' ability to cushion losses without passing them on to depositors. Since 1996, capital adequacy requirements have been considerably strengthened in two-thirds of the countries under review; in five countries a capital adequacy ratio of 10 percent of risk weighted assets has been introduced, and in another four countries a ratio of 8 percent has been introduced.[11] The Basle 8 percent minimum ratio is intended for internationally active banks in an established environment. In countries with a higher risk profile, and with data quality problems, a higher ratio is desirable. Estonia raised the minimum required capital to 10 percent from the previous 8 percent in October 1997, while Lithuania reduced the level to 10 percent from 13 percent effective in early 1997.[12] Risk-weighting tends to follow interna-

[11]Minimum risk-weighted capital adequacy ratios have been brought to 10 percent in Azerbaijan, Belarus, Estonia, Latvia, and Lithuania; in Armenia, the required ratio was expected to increase from 8 percent to 10 percent from the end of September 1998; in Georgia, a gearing ratio of 10 percent has been introduced; Kazakhstan, the Kyrgyz Republic, Turkmenistan, and Uzbekistan have risk-weighted ratios of 8 percent; the remaining five countries have lower required ratios.

[12]The reduction in Lithuania was accompanied by changes in accounting standards that in fact resulted in a tightening of capital requirements.

tional practice; Estonia has raised the risk-weighting of loans to local government institutions and claims guaranteed by local governments to 100 percent, from the previous level of 50 percent.

Average capital adequacy ratios of banks have increased in seven countries.[13] In eight countries the average capital adequacy ratio is 10 percent or higher.[14] In only three countries that have reported an average ratio for 1997 is the actual ratio less than 8 percent.[15] The reported ratios should be regarded with caution, however, because the 15 countries do not always draw clear distinctions between capital and provisions. Loan classification and provisioning regulations, although in place in all countries except Tajikistan, are not always applied correctly by the banks or verified by the supervisors. Capital levels may also be overstated as a result of calculation methods that do not correspond to international practices, and inappropriate underprovisioning practices.

Asset quality is a key indicator of bank soundness.[16] On a simple cross-country average, nonperforming loans as a percentage of total loans are reported to be 10 percent, with a standard deviation of 8 percent (Figure 4.2).[17] In the large majority of countries, asset quality has improved, although concerns persist as to the accuracy of the asset quality data, because of continued weak on-site inspection skills and insufficiently developed accounting practices. The absorption of losses from previous periods has progressed, leading to a lower amount of remaining nonperforming claims. As banks' liquidity management improves and alternative safe investments become available, the large-scale shift made by many banks to investment in low-risk government securities will need to be reduced. In the short term, however, this shift improves the risk profile of bank balance sheets. In Tajikistan and Uzbekistan, the ratio of nonperforming loans to total loans increased in 1997, although in these countries reported loan losses may have risen as a result of the application of more stringent rules on loan classification and provisioning than in previous years.

In the crucial area of loan classification and provisioning, improvements are being introduced in most countries reviewed in this study, although in

[13]Armenia, Georgia, Kyrgyz Republic, Latvia, Tajikistan, Turkmenistan, and Ukraine.

[14]Armenia, Belarus, Estonia, Georgia, Latvia, Lithuania, Turkmenistan, and Ukraine.

[15]Uzbekistan (less than 1 percent), Moldova (6 percent), and Russia (7 percent).

[16]Two basic indicators for asset quality are the level of nonperforming loans to total loans, and the level of specific provisions made by a bank, measured in a time series, and compared to levels in peer group institutions.

[17]In established market-oriented banking systems, levels of more than 10 percent are an indicator of serious distress in the system. Currently, in the United States this figure is estimated at 1 percent; in Southeast Asia, nonperforming loans are estimated at between 10 percent and 20 percent of total loans; in Korea, the official estimate for this figure is 6 percent.

Figure 4.2. Nonperforming Loans, 1995–97
(In percent of total loans)

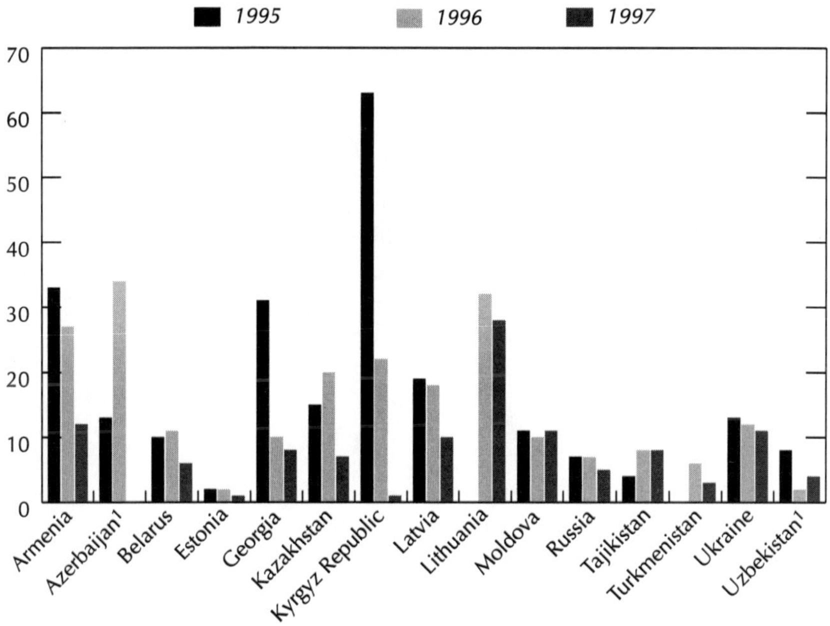

Source: Country authorities.
[1]1995 data not available; 1994 data used.

most cases a simple matrix showing percentages of loans in each category is still applied mechanically on the basis of overdue periods and collateralization.[18] In all countries except Moldova and Tajikistan, interest accrual is suspended on overdue loans. In some countries, such as Russia, an element of supervisory discretion has been introduced that permits bank inspectors to impose higher provisions than suggested by the matrix if the analysis of the payment capacity of the borrower warrants this caution. Systems still remain weak, however, to the extent that banks do not generally have good data for assessing the need for provisioning, and bank supervisors lack skills or resources to verify bank provisioning levels based on their assessment of the payment capacity of borrowers. To develop this capability requires practical experience, although additional training may also be required. Also, because of persistent budgetary problems, full tax

[18]All countries except Tajikistan report having a regulation on loan classification and provisioning.

deductibility of specific provisions has been introduced in only a few countries.

Risk diversification rules are also generally applied, and in most countries limits have been brought down to acceptable international standards. Bank exposure to single borrowers or connected groups of borrowers should not exceed 25 percent of regulatory capital.[19] In some countries, a limit of 20 percent is applied. A weakness in this respect is the insufficient implementation of supervision on a consolidated basis, and therefore the ease with which these regulations can be circumvented. Even more than in established market economies, liquidity is a key concern for banks in the countries under review, and is often given excessive importance by management and supervisory authorities over profitability and long-term solvency. All countries apply liquid asset ratios. Required levels are in the order of 20 percent of short-term obligations.

Other Supervisory Issues

In most countries, licensing requirements stipulate that bank management must have adequate training and banking experience. Clearly, this criterion cannot be isolated from local availabilities. A lack of qualified bankers remains a structural problem in many countries. Credit risk assessment and loan review skills need to be further developed. Limits on lending to shareholders are typically between 10 percent and 20 percent of the bank's regulatory capital, thus limiting conflict of interest between the bank and its shareholder borrowers.[20] Again, because of the risk involved in banking in these countries, this relatively conservative approach, as well as a lower limit than those applied in established market economies, is appropriate. Compliance is difficult to verify, however, in light of continuing weaknesses in consolidated supervision. Lending to insiders—that is, management and related parties—is often strictly regulated on paper but not always strictly enforced in practice in many countries, and may not be higher than a few percent of regulatory capital. The once widely prevalent practice of government directed lending has been suppressed in most countries. As international experience has shown, limitations on bank autonomy with regard to credit allocation tends to lead to poor asset quality.

[19]Regulatory capital is the total of tier I and tier II capital.

[20]Armenia, Azerbaijan, Estonia, Kazakhstan, and Lithuania apply limits of 10 percent (in Armenia, the limit declined to 5 percent at the end of 1998); Belarus, Moldova, and Russia apply a limit of 20 percent, whereas a 15 percent limit is used in the Kyrgyz Republic, Latvia, and Uzbekistan. In Georgia a 50 percent limit is used. The EU, for comparison, limits lending to shareholders to 20 percent of regulatory capital.

Banks in the countries under review still have not established credit allocation policies that are sufficiently strong to prevent renewed asset quality problems or to assure that increased intermediation demands can be handled responsibly. An important issue for the future remains the ability of bankers to price credit risk. Better enterprise accounting and disclosure will be an important factor, as well as increased emphasis on cash-flow-based, rather than collateral-based lending, and improved internal credit review and provisioning procedures.

In the field of accounting and audit, compliance with International Accounting Standards (IAS) is in many cases still in a developmental phase (see also Chapter 6). A specific bottleneck in almost all countries is the lack of consolidated accounts and supervision on a consolidated basis.[21] These missing elements have implications for compliance with most prudential regulations. Supervisors, therefore, cannot sufficiently assess the formal and informal connections of banks and their shareholders, and concomitant connected lending. Although 13 countries report having moved to IAS as the basis for bank accounting and reporting, in most cases, refinements still need to be made and experience gathered.[22] In many countries, financial statements still basically do little more than restructure data collected on the basis of the former accounting system into a format that is compatible with IAS. The underlying ledger data are generally not compiled according to IAS.

In all these countries, banks are obliged to have an internal audit function, and must by law submit their annual financial statements to an external audit. Additionally, banks that participate, for instance, in World Bank banking sector assistance projects, such as the Financial Institution Development Project, must have audits performed on the basis of IAS. In the Baltics, Russia, and other countries of the former Soviet Union, where some banks are beginning to tap international capital markets, banks must be able to present IAS financial statements to their market counterparts, notwithstanding separately structured central bank reporting and accounting systems.

Supervisory authorities have generally introduced basic prudential reporting formats and inspection programs and, in most countries, banks must now submit prudential reports on a monthly basis, and undergo on-site inspections more frequently. Weaknesses persist in the quality of the

[21]Although all countries report that consolidated supervision is applied, this in many cases refers to the consolidation of branches of banks, not of subsidiaries. In any case, implementation is weak, and has generally not enabled supervisors to obtain a clear view of banks' related interests.

[22]All countries except Russia, which has only adopted IAS to some degree, and Tajikistan have moved to International Accounting Standards.

data submitted, the skills of off-site analysts, and the effectiveness of on-site inspections. Quality of analysis will improve with experience, and as longer time series of data become available and better accounting standards are introduced, supervisory authorities will be able to improve their peer group analysis. Inspectors will need to focus on the analysis of borrowers' payment capacity and the adequacy of provisioning levels reported by banks, to correctly establish the bank's net worth.

In all countries except Kazakhstan, the number of supervisory staff relative to the number of banks under supervision has increased since 1997. Absolute numbers of banking supervision staff have increased in six countries, remained stable in six others, and declined slightly in the remainder.[23] As the number of banks has generally decreased, the ratio of supervisory staff per bank has risen. For the coming period, the issue is not only the acquisition of additional numbers of staff—specifically in Azerbaijan, Estonia, Georgia, Tajikistan, Turkmenistan, and Ukraine, where the ratio of staff to the number of banks is relatively low—but the improvement in the quality of staff and the retention of qualified staff.[24]

Working relations between the supervisory authorities and commercial banks still need to be improved. Supervisory authorities have a tendency to issue too many new regulations without sufficient prior consultation, with too great a frequency and too little time to prepare implementation. For their part, commercial banks still need to develop a basic awareness of the underlying common sense of the prudential requirements, and focus on reporting the substance of their operations rather than the form, such as meeting the imposed ratios. Inspection teams still too often include nonsupervisory staff, such as tax inspectors. Under these conditions it is not possible to move from the excessively adversarial relationship that now exists between banks and their supervisors to a more collegial and productive one.

The supervisory authorities in most countries have enjoyed sufficient autonomy to carry out most of their responsibilities. They have been able to conduct bank restructuring policies—mainly of the smaller banks—and to successfully intervene in weak or insolvent banks, imposing temporary administration or closing banks. In a few countries, for instance Moldova, the supervisory authorities' decisions have been challenged in the courts, sometimes successfully. One major shortcoming of the supervisory

[23]Increases were recorded in Georgia, the Kyrgyz Republic, Moldova, Russia, Turkmenistan and Ukraine; numbers remained stable in Azerbaijan, Belarus, Latvia, Lithuania, Tajikistan, and Uzbekistan.

[24]In Armenia, a program of intensive, on-the-job training in U.S. regulatory agencies has been implemented for all supervisors.

authorities in a number of countries has been the hesitancy to deal with the weaknesses in larger institutions. In Russia, the supervisory authorities need to obtain better information on the risks incurred by the large banks that form part of financial-industrial groups. The statutory authority of central banks to close such large banks, should they be found nonviable, needs to be clarified. Liquidations of banks for which the licenses have been withdrawn is a slow and very uneven process in most countries, mainly because there is still too great a dependency on shareholder cooperation in liquidating banks. Moreover, the legislative framework for bank bankruptcy remains very weak.

Country Rankings on Bank Supervision

The 1997 ranking of the quality of banking supervision took into account a range of factors, including (1) the degree to which the basic legal and regulatory framework needed for banking supervision is in place; (2) whether the quality of data can be sufficiently ensured; (3) whether off-site monitoring and on-site inspection capabilities are sufficient; and (4) whether enforcement and intervention powers are adequate. Also included are estimates of the quality of accounting and reporting and the implementation of corrective measures. The rankings for 1998 include an assessment of the progress made during 1997. The rankings provide only an approximation of progress made, since they are based on information that is uneven across countries (see Table 4.3).

Priorities for Reform

Although much progress has been made in bank restructuring and in building the basic framework for banking supervision, there are still a number of unresolved issues regarding the performance of major banks formerly owned by the state. In some countries (including Russia), the central bank still owns major banks, which are used to provide liquidity support to other banks. The bank restructuring process will need to be completed in the next two years or so because a sufficiently large body of healthy banks will need to be in place as growth resumes, confidence returns, and intermediation demands increase. In the post-restructuring phase, banking supervision will need to be ready to deal with the risks to the banking system potentially caused by the expected, and necessary, rapid growth in the ratio of total banking system assets to GDP.[25]

[25]Estonian authorities state that excessive credit growth may outpace the abilities of most commercial banks to prudently assess and price risk.

Table 4.3. Banking Supervision

I Limited Progress	II Moderate Progress	III Substantial Progress
Belarus	Azerbaijan	Armenia
Tajikistan	Turkmenistan	Estonia
	Ukraine	Georgia
	Uzbekistan	Kazakhstan
		Kyrgyz Republic
		Latvia
		Lithuania
		Moldova
		Russia

Although emphasis may differ from country to country, for the group as a whole the following areas are important for the future development of a sound banking system and effective banking supervision.

Bank Restructuring

Priority must now be placed on completion of the restructuring and rehabilitation of the largest banks, since they are crucial for the stability of the system. For many reasons, however, these institutions have been the last to be addressed. This must change so as to obtain a complete view on the risk profile of these institutions, with attention given to the affiliates of the larger banks. In view of the power of these banks, effective measures to restrain imprudent behavior will only be successful if they are firmly based on a pre-established consensus between the political and the supervisory authorities. The supervisory authorities will need to take the initiative in this area. Bank exit policies must be swift and clear if they are to help rebuild confidence in the banking sector. Rules on bank intervention need to be firmly grounded in the relevant laws, which will need to be reviewed to assess their adequacy and effectiveness. In some countries, many banks whose licenses have been revoked remain active, and rules permitting the bankruptcy of banks need to be introduced or reviewed. Expedient and equitable liquidation procedures need to be introduced. Finally, shareholders should not be involved in the liquidation process.

Loan workout remains an issue that many countries see as important. The resolution of nonperforming loans must be accompanied by appropriate measures to restructure the enterprise sector. Most important, banks must develop good skills to assess and price risk.

Banking Supervision

A central concern is the quality of data. Without reliable data, effective supervision is impossible, and banks cannot be run profitably. Improvements in the calculation of capital and capital adequacy are needed, taking into account adequately estimated and verified provisions for nonperforming assets. These improvements are essential for the assessment of the financial soundness of banks. Provisioning should not only be based on loan performance evaluation, but also on forward-looking analyses of the payment capacity of borrowers through an effective cash-flow analysis. Provisioning rules should allow sufficient supervisory discretion in imposing adequate provisioning levels, because standard provisioning matrices do not address questions concerning the payment capacity of debtors. Taxation of specific provisions should be abandoned, since this procedure tends to decapitalize banks. In addition, bank management should consider the further development of techniques for consolidation of accounts and supervision on a consolidated basis so that risks incurred by banks through the activities of their subsidiaries, branches, and other related entities can properly be taken into account.

Rapid adoption of International Accounting Standards that focus on banks' net worth and not on the flow of funds is essential for progress.[26] Key areas are accounting on an accrual basis, the consolidation of accounts, and much greater emphasis on the substance-over-form principle. Again, to help foster a more material rather than a formal compliance-oriented approach to banking supervision, in all countries off-site analysis and on-site inspection skills should focus more on asset quality and provisions, performance, risk diversification, market-risk sensitivity, and connected entities than just on formal compliance. Inspections should also address management quality and internal risk management systems. The more advanced markets, such as those in the Baltics and Russia, will need to address banks' derivative activities in their off-site analysis and inspections. Without better relations between supervisors and banks, effective supervision remains seriously handicapped because of banks' inclinations toward window dressing and other forms of data manipulation. Corrective measures against banks should focus on remedial rather than punitive action, which often leaves the underlying weakness unaddressed. Banking supervision should focus exclusively on issues of bank soundness, and not on quasi-policing or tax inspection functions.

[26]In Armenia (particularly), Azerbaijan, Georgia, Russia (partially), and Tajikistan progress still needs to be made in this area.

5

Payment Systems Development

Nicholas M. Roberts

In addition to facilitating exchanges of goods, services, and financial assets, effective payment systems play a major role in ensuring the soundness of financial systems by limiting the possibility of systemic crises, which could undermine confidence in financial institutions and markets. In the early 1990s, the 15 countries under review were beset with a number of payment system problems. Besides slowness of payment processing, there were, in particular, large interenterprise arrears, defaults, and fraud. A further complication was the breakdown of the ruble area, which caused cash shortages in some countries and excess cash in others, depending on the timing of the introduction of national currencies. The final step in the breakup of the ruble zone occurred in June 1993 when Russia demonetized all pre-1993 ruble bank notes, expediting the departure of the zone's last seven non-Russian members.

Recent Developments

Progress on improving the functioning of domestic payment systems in these countries has subsequently been quite impressive, and in 1997 a number of the countries made concrete progress toward improving their handling of high-value payments.[1] Further progress is needed, however, to bolster financial system stability through the introduction of systemic risk controls and, in particular, real-time gross settlement systems. Also, much remains to be done before the majority of consumers in these countries have a variety of payment methods at their disposal—such as checks, credit cards, debit cards, charge cards, automated clearinghouses, and giro

[1]Details on the features of the payment systems in individual countries are provided in Chapter 8, Table 8.9.

services—and have a choice of competing service providers comparable to those available in mature market economies.

Payment System Risk Management

Since the beginning of the structural transition, most of the countries in this study have focused their efforts involving payment systems on building a risk management framework to encourage sound banking practices and to support the development of financial markets. The quality and degree of commitment to these strategies vary. The development of a reform strategy has suffered for a number of reasons, including the fact that the reforms themselves have only been recently implemented and need to be further developed, as in Azerbaijan, Uzbekistan, and Turkmenistan, or the lack of commitment of the central bank to reform of the payment system. Where a strategy is not solidly supported at senior levels of the central bank, attention tends to shift toward efficiency of payment systems at the expense of risk management objectives, so that the implicit guarantee from the central bank to underwrite bank settlement obligations is confirmed and the associated moral hazard issues are aggravated.

For central banks, a key objective is to ensure that commercial banks have incentives to limit and control their payment exposure to reduce credit risks, and to reduce liquidity risks. Meeting this objective requires that banks settle for their own obligations at regular intervals (at least once a day) and that in doing so they stay within the level of reserves provided by the central bank to the market without recourse to credit from the central bank.

Countries that do not enforce strict discipline at settlement weaken the soundness of their banking sectors because weak banks are not detected early enough and the central bank and commercial banks may incur substantial credit exposures to them. Sound settlement policies help to expose weak banks, limit the systemic impact of a single bank's failure, and thus provide a framework in which exit policies for weak banks can be enforced with the least cost to the public purse.

Countries where settlement discipline needs improvement include Tajikistan and Turkmenistan, where banks may still overdraw their settlement accounts without prior contact with the central bank. These overdrafts occur despite policies in place to prevent banks' automatic access to overdrafts, and despite ex post penalties for overdrawings. The countries under currency board arrangements—Estonia and Lithuania—are constrained by these arrangements to offer only limited credit to banks for settlement purposes, with the total amount of available credit depending on the amount of foreign exchange in excess of the central bank's monetary liabilities.

The countries in this study are now well aware that international best practice in mature market economies is to develop specialized large-value transfer systems to handle the bulk of a country's high-value payments and that most of these systems are designed to operate as real-time gross settlement systems under the control of the central bank. Discussions on the specific form that such systems should take are still ongoing in most of the countries.

Systems similar to real-time gross settlement systems for large and time-sensitive payments are already operating in Belarus and Kazakhstan, while in Russia an embryonic real-time gross settlement system limited to a few banks is being tested. Eight other countries (Armenia, Estonia, Georgia, Kyrgyz Republic, Latvia, Lithuania, Moldova, and Ukraine) are planning real-time gross settlement systems.

Real-time gross settlement systems allow intraday settlement, and the development of such systems can facilitate more efficient delivery-versus-payment arrangements through links to securities transfer systems. This allows a considerable reduction in the risks attached to securities trading and is a priority area for reform in countries with developing securities markets. The countries that are operating delivery-versus-payment systems are: Estonia, Kazakhstan, the Kyrgyz Republic, Latvia, Lithuania, Russia, and Uzbekistan.

Liquidity Management

Settlement policies may help banks to better manage liquidity, in addition to supporting risk management objectives. In support of improved liquidity management, most central banks have adopted the objective of account consolidation, both conceptually and physically. In Armenia, Belarus, Estonia, the Kyrgyz Republic, Latvia, Lithuania, Moldova, Turkmenistan, and almost all banks in Kazakhstan and Ukraine, commercial banks have a single national settlement account with the central bank, while in Georgia, Russia, and Tajikistan banks have, or are moving toward, one account per region. Account holding is still highly dispersed in Azerbaijan, with each branch of every bank having an account with the central bank's head office, and in Uzbekistan bank branches hold accounts with regional offices of the central bank. Plans to further rationalize account holdings are being implemented in Azerbaijan, Kazakhstan, Russia, and Uzbekistan.

Efficiency

In some of the 15 countries under review, the ratio of currency to GDP (Table 5.1) appears to have declined, suggesting that the noncash payment system is increasingly used to make payments.[2]

[2]Data on foreign currency deposits do not indicate an increase in dollarization.

Table 5.1. Currency-to-GDP Ratios in Selected Countries
(In percent)

Country	1994	1996
Belarus	4	3
Kyrgyz Republic	12	11
Latvia	17	15
Lithuania	16	11
Russia	6	5
Ukraine	7	5

Source: Country authorities; and IMF.

Reduced delays and variability in clearing times also indicate an improvement in payment system efficiency. This boost in efficiency has led to the increased use of payment orders. Central banks have automated payment order processing, and clearing times in eight of the countries—Belarus, Estonia, Kazakhstan, Latvia, Lithuania, Moldova, Ukraine, and Uzbekistan—are now short and predictable. In Ukraine and Uzbekistan, the majority of payments are cleared within one day—a remarkable achievement and encouraging contrast to their performance in 1993 when the ruble zone broke up and clearing times often extended to a week or more. Countries that continue to experience delays in clearing are Armenia, Azerbaijan, Georgia, the Kyrgyz Republic, Russia, Tajikistan, and Turkmenistan. In Russia and Kazakhstan, the delays mostly reflect the difficulties of processing payments from and between remote areas and do not appear to affect the bulk of payments that are undertaken within the major business areas of the countries.

In the absence of any initiatives from commercial banks to develop payment services, central banks have taken a lead role in offering improved clearing services in most of the countries under review. In an attempt to stimulate private sector involvement in clearing, some of the central banks in these 15 countries have begun to price their services. In Russia, the pricing of central bank services is also seen as providing an appropriate incentive to commercial banks to develop such services as private clearinghouses and to seek improvements to existing and proposed central bank services. Kazakhstan and Ukraine are also pricing central bank services to encourage private sector involvement in the provision of payment services.

Legal Issues

A particular concern in many of the countries in this study is the failure to reap all the efficiency gains expected from the introduction of electronic processing of payment orders. Countries have been thwarted by the continued need to produce paper documents as evidence of transactions. Paper records are necessary in the event of disputes because current laws require that payments be in writing to be enforceable in court. Countries that are currently running parallel paper and electronic payments because of legal uncertainties surrounding electronic payments include Belarus, Russia, and Ukraine. Countries that have dispensed with parallel paper processing include Estonia and Kazakhstan.

Increasingly, the 15 countries are introducing public or private clearinghouses that rely on multilateral netting of clearing obligations. This innovation allows for a single settlement entry for each party to the netting agreement. As in market economies, the legal status of netting agreements will need to be specifically dealt with in law to avoid the danger that a failed participant, or its liquidator, could try to set aside the netting and accept the full amounts of incoming transfers, while treating the full amounts of outgoing transfers as unsecured obligations. Bankruptcy laws and laws on collateral must also be carefully drafted to avoid undermining payment systems arrangements (see Chapter 7).

Country Rankings

The most advanced countries—Belarus, Estonia, Kazakhstan, Kyrgyz Republic, Latvia, Lithuania, Russia, and Ukraine (Group III)—have made substantial progress in all the major reform areas and have a strong core of payment system expertise within their central banks. In these countries, strategic issues have largely been resolved and problems of implementation and of a technical and operational nature remain. The Group III countries (Table 5.2) have by and large developed enough contacts with central banks and others outside the 15 countries under review to pursue further reforms by making only selective calls for highly focused and specialized technical assistance. They have implemented significant reforms across all areas of their payment systems and have a strong core of personnel capable of guiding future payment system development. Russia has made considerable progress over the past year. A reform strategy was released to the public in April 1997 and, as an interim measure before the introduction of a real-time gross settlement system, Russia has moved to increase the frequency of settlements of payments (the so-called session-settlement model) and introduced several supporting reforms to help banks manage liquidity and risk. Also, as a precursor to a full-scale real-time gross settlement system some Moscow banks have begun operations through the central bank. In Kazakhstan, there has been progress in developing the risk management framework for such an electronic payment system, consolidating accounts held by banks with the central bank,

Table 5.2. Progress in Payment System Policy

I Limited Progress	II Moderate Progress	III Substantial Progress
Tajikistan	Armenia Azerbaijan Georgia Moldova Turkmenistan Uzbekistan	Belarus Estonia Kazakhstan Kyrgyz Republic Latvia Lithunia Russia Ukraine

pricing services, and encouraging private sector participation in payment system development.

Group II countries—Armenia, Azerbaijan, Georgia, Moldova, Turkmenistan, and Uzbekistan—have made substantial progress in several of the major areas of reform and have generally identified the appropriate objectives for further payments reform. Most of the advice that these countries need is more practical than strategic and will often be available from experts who are helping with specific projects that are being, or are soon to be, implemented. Some important decisions on strategy are still required before the final shape of the payment system is consolidated in these countries. While Moldova had made good early progress in 1993 and 1994 and has a working payment system, there is no explicit strategic framework to drive plans for an electronic large-value transfer system or to improve risk management in existing systems. In Georgia there are plans to introduce a platform for processing payments electronically, but the plans to develop this system as a specialized high-value payment system are still under review.

The only country where there has clearly been little progress over the past five years is Tajikistan, where security and political developments have hindered any substantive initiatives.

Priorities for Reform

Payment system reform is an ongoing process in countries throughout the world, and the accepted standards of best practices for payment systems have changed significantly as the awareness and understanding of payment system issues has grown. In the years that the economies of these 15 countries have been in transition from centrally planned to market-based economies, payment reforms in the mature market-based economies have been considerable, with the development of real-time gross settlement systems being a widespread response to the need to reduce risks in the face of growing globalized financial markets.

For the 15 countries in this study, the reform agenda needs to take account of the developments that are driving priorities in the rest of the world, such as improvements to foreign exchange settlement practices and the development of electronic money. Clearly, however, there are more fundamental developmental objectives that need to be met in these countries in addition to the objectives that are relevant in the mature market economies.

The experience of the countries under review since 1992 suggests that developmental reforms tend to proceed in stages. For a country at the beginning of the reform process, as Tajikistan is now, the first priority is to develop an institutional framework to support reform and to use this framework to develop a reform strategy. These steps require developing the central bank's policymaking capabilities and strengthening its link with the private sector through forums such as national payment system councils. At this stage, experts from central banks are the most appropriate source of advice.

The initial goals of reform will normally give priority to amending the existing payment system structure after it has been thoroughly analyzed and the main shortcomings exposed. At this stage most of the countries reviewed in this volume have started to embark on automation projects to support processing of payment orders, and restructured the central bank and its payment operations. The six countries in Group II have reached this phase, but they have not committed to reforms that will be needed to support financial stability once financial markets and the banking sector start to grow significantly. In this phase central bank experts from countries with reform experience are very helpful.

The countries in Group III for the most part now operate reasonably efficient payment systems and have committed to such important reforms as real-time gross settlement systems, which will support growth in financial markets as it occurs. For these countries, the expertise required tends to become specific and technical as individual projects are implemented. At this point, there is less certainty that central bank "policy experts" will have all the necessary technical expertise required by the countries in this study, although such experts may still be useful in coordinating different projects and in explaining the implications and overlaps of payment system changes for the whole range of the central bank's activities.

Underlying this sequence of reforms is the need for fundamental changes in legal infrastructure and in the skills of the finance industry, which may take time and patience to develop. To see this take place, two deep-rooted changes must occur—the private sector should develop to a level where it can provide high-quality retail and wholesale payment services and the legal system must reach a level where there is a satisfactory degree of certainty attached to payment transactions. Not surprisingly, the existing legal systems in the countries under review are not yet well adapted to supporting modern payment systems, with the result that there is a considerable task ahead. In developed market economies, payment system rules have developed over many years from private agreements to detailed statutory rules. It may be a mistake for a country that has just recently developed as a market economy to establish detailed statutory rules before the needs of the participants are clearly understood.

Initially, rules for payment systems may best be located in interbank agreements rather than in statutes. These agreements may be replaced by regulations or a statute as the size and importance of the payment system increase and stabilize. Ultimately, the rules for a mature payment system may best be established by statute.

Countries where these more fundamental and intractable issues are moving to the forefront are more likely to find answers from their own central banks rather than outside experts as they continuously monitor emerging trends and develop understanding of the particular problems faced in their own countries. In terms of technical assistance needs, the only country that still needs the type of extensive advice offered to the countries at the start of their transition toward market-based economies is Tajikistan. There, the fundamentals of allocating staff in the central bank to payment issues, starting consultations with banks, and developing an understanding of what may be involved in payment system reform are still priorities.

Some of the Group II countries are close to achieving significant efficiency gains through electronic processing of payment orders, and have largely completed account consolidation projects and established reasonable central bank discipline over the credit facilities available to banks. These countries now need to develop forward-looking plans to provide upgraded risk management to support expanded financial and other market activities. There are sufficient staff in the central banks of these countries to do this job themselves, but they are still likely to benefit from regular exposure to the experiences of the 15 countries and mature market economies. One model for encouraging exposure to outside experiences is through regular forums such as the payment system workshops organized by the IMF's Monetary and Exchange Affairs department. Another possibility is to establish a panel of outside advisors, as has been done in Russia in the form of the International Steering Committee. In addition, various countries may need outside experts to provide specific technical advice as general proposals need to be turned into concrete projects.

For those countries where progress with reform has been only a relatively recent development—such as Azerbaijan, Georgia, and Turkmenistan—certain strategic issues, while apparently resolved, may still need to be reaffirmed by outside experts on a continuing basis to prevent backtracking.

The remaining challenges for all 15 countries are the development of policies that encourage the growth of competition and innovation in private sector provision of payment services. Central banks will need to encourage commercial banks to play an increasing role in the payment system, and the legal and regulatory framework must be modified to promote confidence in payment instruments and clearing and settlement arrangements.

6

Central Bank Accounting and Internal Audit

John Dalton

The range of basic central bank accounting reforms adopted by the Baltics, Russia, and other countries of the former Soviet Union underscores the importance of reliable financial information in the effective conduct of market-based monetary and exchange market operations. With recent efforts by Azerbaijan, Kyrgyz Republic, and Ukraine, 11 central banks have introduced accounting systems that are broadly consistent with International Accounting Standards (IAS). Together with the information needed in a market economy, these systems promise to provide central bank managers with the financial information needed to inform policy deliberations as well as public financial statements. In nearly all of these cases, the reliability of the financial information produced by these new systems has also been subjected to varying degrees of independent assessment by internationally qualified external auditors. As part of the new accounting systems, the internal controls used by central banks to maintain the integrity of accounting information have been improved. Table 6.1 summarizes accounting reforms for each country during 1992–97.

Internal audit reform has received less attention and has thus far proceeded at a slower rate of progress. The objective of reform in this area has been to promote the creation of independent audit departments with responsibility for reviewing the operation and effectiveness of management control systems used to limit or reduce key risks faced by central banks. Efforts in this area have gained momentum in the past two years in at least two-thirds of the 15 countries under review.

Recent Developments

Five countries—Armenia, Estonia, Latvia, Lithuania, and Kazakhstan—have now introduced central bank accounting systems that are consistent

Table 6.1. Central Bank Accounting Reforms, 1992–97

	New Chart of Accounts Introduced	Accruals Basis Adopted	International Accounting Standards (IAS) External Audits (1995–97)[1]
Armenia	January 1996	Yes	Yes (1995–97)
Azerbaijan	February 1997	Yes	Yes (1996)
Belarus	January 1996	Yes	Yes (1996)
Estonia	1993	Yes	Yes (1993–97)
Georgia	January 1996	Yes	Yes (1996–97)
Kazakhstan	January 1997	Yes	Yes (1996–97)
Kyrgyz Republic	April 1997	Yes	Yes (1995–97)
Latvia	1993	Yes	Yes (1993–97)
Lithuania	1993	Yes	Yes (1994–97)
Moldova	1995	Yes	No
Russia	January 1998	No	No[2]
Tajikistan	New chart not yet introduced	No	No
Turkmenistan	March 1998	Yes	No
Ukraine	February 1998	Yes	Yes (1995–96)[3]
Uzbekistan	March 1997	Yes	No

Source: IMF staff.
[1]The first year shown refers to limited audit of closing balances only.
[2]Diagnostic audits were made for 1993–95 accounts.
[3]Qualified opinion.

with IAS, and have also undergone a full external audit of their financial statements.[1] Each has demonstrated a clear ability to develop and implement accounting reforms that have enabled the central bank to introduce more transparent and fuller disclosure of accounting information and to lead the way in building confidence in the financial sector. The Baltic countries are the most experienced, having received "clean" audit reports from internationally qualified auditors since 1994. Armenia and Kazakhstan have more recently moved into the annual audit cycle.

During 1997–98, another six countries—Azerbaijan, Belarus, Georgia, Kyrgyz Republic, Moldova, and Ukraine—continued to progress in their adoption of a range of basic accounting reforms, including implementa-

[1]A full external audit in this context refers to an audit that expresses an opinion on the accounts for the whole year. It attests to the truth and fairness of the opening and closing balances, as well as the integrity of the accounts and records. This type of audit differs from the more limited audit of end-year balances only. For the 15 countries, the limited audit has typically occurred when a bank's financial accounts have been audited for the first time. In this instance, the certification of closing balances sets a basis for a full audit in the following year.

tion of a chart of accounts that permits compilation of accounting reports and IAS-consistent financial statements. Each of these, however, needs to take some additional steps to complete the basic reform process. Generally these steps are required because various countries have not fully adopted IAS-based principles, or they have not completely implemented new systems. In Georgia, for example, policies are consistent with IAS, but further systems work is necessary to enable the new chart of accounts to be used for recording transactions at the detailed or analytical account level. In Ukraine, IAS-compliant financial statements were produced for 1996, and a new chart became operational at the head office level in February 1998, but consolidation of branch data on the same basis is still to come. In the Kyrgyz Republic, live operation of the new chart has commenced, but further work is required to enable compilation of data for inclusion in the IMF's *International Financial Statistics*. In Moldova, the central bank adopted accrual-based accounting in January 1998. IAS were also adopted economywide from that date.

Progress in the reform of internal audit procedures in the 11 countries noted in the previous two paragraphs is mixed, but all have recognized the need for internal audit policies and practices that can be used to assess key risk areas in market-based central bank operations. Countries that have made more notable progress are Belarus and Kazakhstan. The National Bank of Kazakhstan, for example, has drafted a set of auditing standards that focus on identifying the main risk areas of operations, audit responsibilities, management responsibilities for internal controls, planning and scheduling of audits, and requisite staff qualifications.

Countries that have shown less progress in the implementation of accounting reform—Russia, Tajikistan, Turkmenistan, and Uzbekistan—have nonetheless made some gains. Uzbekistan in March 1997 and Turkmenistan in early 1998 each introduced a new central bank chart of accounts that more closely reflects market-based operations and adopts the accrual principle.

In Russia, a new central bank chart of accounts came into operation in January 1998, but it does not fully adopt the accrual principle, on which IAS are based. Financial statements compiled from the chart are not in a form or content that is consistent with the requirements of IAS, nor has an IAS external audit been conducted. The failure to adopt the accrual principle is a particular concern to professional accountants. It also has implications for commercial bank accounting reform, given the central bank's key role in specifying the chart of accounts and related instructions for commercial banks. Objections have been raised to the adoption of the accrual principle by commercial banks in part because the tax system is not consistent with such treatment, and partially because commercial banks might misapply the principle where nonperforming loans are concerned.[2] The Central Bank of Russia has identified this inconsistency as a future reform issue resolution in the transition from cash to accrual accounting.

Turkmenistan and Uzbekistan have now implemented a new chart of accounts. The Uzbekistan authorities believe that the new chart is broadly consistent with IAS. In Turkmenistan, implementation was set to begin in early 1998 with parallel operation of both new and old charts. Both countries have yet to complete an external audit by an internationally-recognized auditor. Tajikistan has received some initial guidance on reform work and has indicated a commitment to reform, but plans continue to be hampered by unsettled conditions in the country—thus progress can be classified only as very limited.

Consistent with the slower rate of progress on accounting issues, internal audit reform in Russia, Tajikistan, Turkmenistan, and Uzbekistan has been modest at best. With the exception of Russia, where resources have been devoted to auditing the large branch structure, the internal audit function in the other three countries largely remains focused on the traditional areas of operation such as cash handling and payment processing, and on detailed checking of all transactions.

Country Rankings

Table 6.2 provides an overall ranking of progress by individual countries in their implementation of central bank accounting and audit reforms. As indicated by the discussion of recent developments, more than two-thirds of the countries under review are now regarded as having made substantial progress.

While individual experiences differ, countries included in Group III have generally reached the stage of reform where a new chart of accounts based on the principles underlying IAS has been adopted and is being used as the basis for the preparation of financial statements. In almost all cases there has also been an external audit examination by an internationally recognized auditor. One particular distinguishing feature is that these countries have overcome some of the earlier conceptual and practical impediments to reform that confronted them initially. These obstacles

[2]There is a concern that income would be overstated because accrual accounting recognizes interest income when it is due and not when it is received. Thus when interest is later found to be uncollectible, income has already been measured. Accrual procedures have mechanisms to avoid such overstatement by, for example, cessation of interest accrual (for income determination purposes) once a loan is more than 90 days overdue; by reversal of previously accrued income when interest is more than 180 days overdue; and, if necessary, provisioning against interest previously capitalized as part of a borrowers' indebtedness.

Table 6.2. Progress in Central Bank Accounting and Internal Audit

I Limited Progress	II Moderate Progress	III Substantial Progress
Tajikistan	Russia	Armenia
	Turkmenistan	Azerbaijan
	Uzbekistan	Belarus
		Estonia
		Georgia
		Kazakhstan
		Kyrgyz Republic
		Latvia
		Lithuania
		Moldova
		Ukraine

included acceptance of basic principles relating to the accrual principle and asset valuation, as well as developing or acquiring adequate computer systems to support accounting processing and reporting.

Countries in Group II, while having made progress in the development of new charts of accounts, have yet to translate this developmental work into practical application through testing or limited operation, or financial statement formats reflecting a new chart. In particular, financial statements have not been subject to an official audit by internationally qualified auditors that included an opinion on the statements. In Russia, however, external auditors have made several annual diagnostic audits of the central bank's accounts.

Priorities for Reform

Notwithstanding the substantial progress achieved by many countries, a range of technical issues remain to be addressed if each country is to develop central bank accounting and audit procedures that reflect best international practices, and to ensure the constant availability of reliable, transparent, and fully disclosed financial information.[3]

For the more advanced (Group III) countries, reform issues for central banks involve:

- enhancing accounting control and information systems to support effective management of central bank resources;

[3]Important reform issues of relevance for individual countries are summarized in Chapter 8, Table 8.10.

- establishing policies for the maintenance of central bank financial soundness; and
- promoting financial discipline through the central bank, which should take a lead role in establishing full and transparent disclosure standards for its own financial statements.

For those countries that have made significant progress but are still in the final stages of implementing new accounting systems, additional reform issues include addressing technical aspects associated with the installation of new computerized accounts processing systems, and further developing appropriate controls to ensure the integrity and security of those systems.

For those countries that have experienced only moderate (Group II) or limited progress (Group I), reform issues require the delivery of the fundamental principles on which IAS accounting are based, including the accounting procedures associated with implementation of a chart of accounts for market-based central bank operations. Additional steps may also require removing legislative obstacles to the adoption of accrual-based accounting or the appointment of external auditors who are not nationals of the country concerned. Until these countries can address these basic issues they will not have the capability to produce regular, reliable, and comparable financial information that provides a sound basis for policy actions and financial sector surveillance.

Additional issues of relevance for all countries include:

- adoption of accounting policies and procedures, and internal controls for central bank operations involving new financial instruments, especially those involving off-balance sheet activities;
- more structured staff training and development programs to improve central banks' own internal capacity in accounting and audit, and to reduce reliance on external advisors for assistance with day-to-day problems;
- addressing control and operational problems associated with the use of new technologies, including resolution of Year 2000 date change issues;
- development of internal audit systems that are responsible for assessing the effectiveness of internal controls, as set by management, in limiting the risks faced in market-based central bank operations; and
- harmonization of overall central bank and financial sector accounting and reporting standards generally.[4]

[4]This important issue must not be confused with the differences that exist between, for example, central bank and commercial bank operations. Both can follow broadly similar standards, since this promotes better understanding by the general public and financial specialists. To the extent that differences exist in operations, these issues can best be covered not by different standards, or by failure to adopt standards, but by full and transparent disclosure of the respective operations.

One further related issue of importance concerns the role central banks can play in promoting commercial bank accounting reforms that are consistent with IAS. In the 15 countries reviewed in this study, central banks have been responsible for issuing accounting standards and instructions for commercial bank accounting generally, and for the collection of financial information for economic, prudential, and financial market surveillance purposes. The adoption of commercial bank accounting standards that are consistent with IAS is a key factor in achieving transparency in commercial bank financial reporting and in developing well-functioning financial markets and sound banking systems.

The stages reached by central banks in individual countries, and future issues, have particular implications for coordinated technical assistance. For instance, the Baltic states and Armenia, listed in Group III of Table 6.2, might now be regarded as no longer requiring assistance on accounting reform issues through the IMF's Monetary and Exchange Affairs (MAE) department-coordinated program. However, this should not preclude future requests to the IMF for technical assistance on the issues they have identified, or for any other specific technical issue that may arise. For the other countries with substantial progress to their credit, expert involvement in technical assistance can be expected to be by way of short-term visits on an occasional basis, with the length of visits varying across individual countries.

In countries showing moderate progress, some combination of short-term or, possibly, longer-term assignments probably would be necessary, particularly where countries see a clear benefit in committing to an implementation program and use of cooperating central bank experts. Since a program might be expected to take two to three years, the support of a cooperating central bank can provide continuity to a project even if individual experts have to change. In Tajikistan, intensive assistance will be necessary, and likely to require substantial on-site-based advice from a longer-term expert.

7

Legislative Framework

Tonny Lybek

The reform efforts outlined in the previous chapters must be supported by an appropriate legal framework; that is, one that enforces economic decisions made based on market principles.

Recent Developments

Since the end of 1991, the 15 countries under review have generally achieved significant progress in establishing a sound legal framework for central banks and commercial banks. Some progress has also been made in legislation supporting banking transactions. Laws governing contracts, collateral, and bankruptcy have been passed, but legal uncertainties about the enforceability of these laws may continue to contribute to the generally large spread between lending and deposit rates for financial institutions in most of the 15 countries.

Central Bank Legislation

It is now generally accepted in advanced market economies that price stability with a medium-term focus should be the primary objective of a central bank. Central bank reforms over the last decade have concentrated on the need to assign the central bank the appropriate autonomy in support of this objective. Although it is the prerogative of the state to conduct monetary policy, the government normally has many different objectives. Some of these objectives may be at odds with a medium-term approach and may result in a short-term monetary policy with an inflationary basis, which hampers sustainable growth. Experience shows that delegating the authority over monetary policy—or at a minimum the implementation of monetary policy—to an autonomous central bank can improve the credibility of monetary policy. As a counterpart of this delegation of authority, however, a central bank must ensure that its transactions are transparent and that information is disclosed on a regular basis so that it may be held accountable for its performance. The linkage with the primary objective, together with appropriate coordination between autonomy and accountability, further enhances the credibility of monetary policy.

The Baltics, Russia, and other countries of the former Soviet Union have made significant progress in establishing a sound institutional framework by adopting central bank laws that generally ensure a medium-term focus on price stability and that shield the central bank from the short-term objectives of the government (the time-inconsistency problem). The central bank law established in the Kyrgyz Republic in 1997 is a noteworthy example of how to do this. In particular, this law has incorporated the primary objective of price stability while at the same time establishing central bank political and economic autonomy to implement policies in support of this objective. Moreover, autonomy is balanced by appropriate accountability provisions. The countries under review have also made a great deal of progress in this area. Three countries—Kazakhstan, Kyrgyz Republic, and Lithuania—introduced amendments to their central bank laws in 1997 (Table 7.1). As mentioned, the amendments introduced by the Kyrgyz Republic were comprehensive, and brought the law fully in line with modern standards. In Kazakhstan, the law was already broadly appropriate, but the amendment underscored the important principle that the National Bank of Kazakhstan is prohibited from extending direct credit to the government. The amendment to the central bank law of Lithuania was relatively minor, relating to the enforceability of collateral pledged to the Bank of Lithuania. Five countries—Belarus, Estonia, Latvia, Lithuania, and Ukraine—are in the process of modifying their central bank law. In Estonia, Latvia, and Lithuania, amendments are intended to further entrench the central bank's autonomy and accountability. Ukraine is now in the process of developing a comprehensive amendment to its 1991 law to bring it into conformity with modern standards. In Belarus, however, some of the recently proposed amendments to the law of 1995 may, in fact, reduce the national bank's autonomy.

In the following section, central bank laws in the countries under study are assessed against four key criteria: primary objective of price stability, political autonomy, economic autonomy, and accountability.[1] This assess-

[1]Sound policy formulation means that the central bank can formulate and implement monetary policy consistent with the exchange rate policy and that provisions are in place for coordination and resolution of conflicts with the government. Political autonomy safeguards

Table 7.1. Amendments of Central Bank Legislation
(Until the end of 1997)

Country	Earlier Amendments of Central Bank Legislation	Most Recent Amendment (Date of Adoption)	Currently Under Review
Armenia	1992, 1993, and 1995	June 1996	No
Azerbaijan	1992	June 1996	No
Belarus	1990, 1992, 1993, 1994, and 1995	March 1995	Yes[1]
Estonia	1990 and 1993	April 1994	Yes[2]
Georgia	1991, 1993, and 1995	May 1996	No
Kazakhstan	1991, 1993, and 1995	July 1997	No
Kyrgyz Republic	1991 and 1992	July 1997	No
Latvia	1990 and 1992	June 1997	Yes[2]
Lithuania	1990, 1994, and 1996	April 1997	Yes[2]
Moldova	1991, 1992, and 1994	September 1995	No
Russia	1990, 1992, 1993, 1995, and 1996	April 1997	Yes
Tajikistan	1991, 1993, and 1995	December 1996	No
Turkmenistan	1992	October 1993	No
Ukraine	1990	March 1991	Yes[3]
Uzbekistan	1991 and 1992	December 1995	No

Source: IMF staff.
[1]The draft banking code is currently being reviewed by the Budget and Finance Commission of the House of Representatives.
[2]Central bank legislation has been amended with a view to achieving consistency with the future European System of Central Banks.
[3]Draft central bank law considered for first reading by parliament in October 1997.

ment is based on the laws as written. Anecdotal evidence suggests that key provisions may be overridden in practice in some countries.[2]

Objectives

Clearly defined objectives in the central bank law are important, as they give the bank implied authority to achieve these goals and provide a more precise basis for holding it accountable. Most authorities recognize price

the bank's governing bodies from short-term political influence by way of sound provisions for the appointment, term, and dismissal of members of these bodies. Economic autonomy ensures that the central bank can actually manage the liquidity in the banking system through explicit limits on prohibitions against providing direct credit to the government and quasi-fiscal activities and that the bank is in solid financial condition. Accountability implies that the central bank will regularly report and publish transparent information on its monetary policy and financial condition.

[2]For example, profit allocation in Russia and directed credit at subsidized interest rates to the agricultural sector in Turkmenistan.

stability as the primary objective, since experience has shown this to be conducive to sustainable real growth. With that realization, 11 of the 15 countries in this study have made price stability the primary objective of their central banks, either explicitly or by linking the currency to an anchor currency.[3] In the remaining countries, price stability is mentioned among other objectives—Azerbaijan, Russia, and Turkmenistan—or indirectly by stipulating monetary or currency stability as one of the objectives, as in Ukraine.

Political Autonomy

As part of the autonomy discussed above, central bank governing bodies should be shielded from the government's short-term influence on the implementation of monetary policy. The governor of the central bank is responsible for implementing monetary policy and should thus be made immune from potential day-to-day political influence. The governor is also often (with the exception of Estonia and Latvia) the chairman of the board and therefore has significant influence on the decisions of the central bank, even though the power may formally rest with the entire board. A so-called double-veto arrangement for appointments, where one party's nomination is subject to approval by another arm of government (presuming the various entities do in fact balance one another) can strengthen the governor's credibility. In almost half of the countries under review—Armenia, Estonia, Georgia, Kazakhstan, Lithuania, Russia, and Uzbekistan—the head of state nominates the governor of the central bank, who then is appointed by the legislature. In Belarus, the Kyrgyz Republic, and Tajikistan, however, the president appoints the chairman with the consent of the legislature. In two countries—Moldova and Ukraine—the legislature appoints the governor, but upon recommendation of the chairman of the legislature. The governor in Latvia is appointed by secret ballot in parliament upon recommendation of at least ten parliamentary members. In Azerbaijan, the chairman is appointed by the president from members of the board. There is no double-veto arrangement in Turkmenistan, where the president appoints the governor.

To avoid subjecting the governor to political pressure, the term should be longer than the political election cycle of the bodies nominating and appointing the governor (generally four years). For instance, in the 15 countries in this study, the respective governors' terms range between four

[3]Both Estonia and Lithuania operate under a currency board arrangement, which implies a clearly defined objective.

and seven years.[4] The laws covering terms should avoid subjecting the governor to uncertainty of a possible dismissal over conflicts on monetary policy. Removal from office should only take place in extreme cases of breaches of qualification requirements, misconduct, and, if it can be clearly defined, poor performance. With the exception of Azerbaijan, Belarus, Kazakhstan, and Ukraine, the countries in the study have some provision in their respective banking laws that generally protects the governor from arbitrary dismissal. Some countries stipulate that dismissal can only take place for breaches of qualification requirements or only after a conviction in court.[5]

The boards of directors of central banks in the countries being reviewed have an important role in formulating monetary policy and in monitoring the central bank's implementation and its financial condition. The composition of the board is therefore important for the autonomy of the central bank. The number of board members varies from 5 to 14.[6] In most countries—except, for example, Armenia, where the president appoints the board members—a double-veto arrangement governs the appointment of board members.[7] In about half of the countries, the legislature appoints the members, either upon recommendation or nomination by the head of state, as in Azerbaijan, Georgia, and Russia, or the governor, as in Estonia, Lithuania, Moldova, Ukraine, and Uzbekistan. The head of state appoints the members with the consent of the legislature in Belarus. In Kazakhstan, the president, the Supreme Council, and the Cabinet each appoint different board members—with the exception of the chairman, who is appointed by the Supreme Council on the recommendation of the president.

[4]Term of governors: seven years in Armenia, Georgia, Kyrgyz Republic, Moldova, and Turkmenistan; six years in Belarus, Kazakhstan, and Latvia; five years in Azerbaijan, Estonia, Lithuania, and Uzbekistan; and four years in Russia. Two countries—Tajikistan and Ukraine—have not explicitly defined a term in the central bank law. In general, longer terms should allow dismissal not just for misconduct, but also for poor performance, if the latter can be clearly defined.

[5]Ideally, accusations of misconduct should be allowed to be ruled upon by a court or by a special tribunal to avoid arbitrary dismissals, or, at a minimum, be approved or made known to the legislature.

[6]The number of board members in the transition countries is: five in Moldova and Tajikistan; seven in Armenia and Azerbaijan; eight in Latvia; nine in Estonia, Georgia, Kazakhstan, and the Kyrgyz Republic; 11 in Uzbekistan; 13 in Russia; and 14 in Lithuania. In Ukraine, a specific number is not stipulated, but according to the current draft, the Council of the Bank of Ukraine will include 14 members. The number of board members is not specified in Belarus.

[7]Nevertheless, board members are explicitly required to act in accordance with the statutory objectives of the Central Bank of Armenia.

To protect the autonomy of board members, the board's term should be longer than the election cycle and the terms of its members should be staggered so as to ensure continuity of policy.[8] Sound provisions that prevent arbitrary removal of board members are in place in Estonia, Georgia, the Kyrgyz Republic, Latvia, Lithuania, and Moldova.

Economic Autonomy

A basic principle of the legal framework for a modern central bank is that the law should protect the central bank's authority over monetary policy from government encroachment. In the countries studied in this volume, a few prohibit direct credit to the government, either explicitly in the central bank law, as, for instance, in the Kyrgyz Republic, or implicitly due to a currency board arrangement, as in Estonia and Lithuania. In other countries—Armenia, Belarus, Georgia, Latvia, Tajikistan, and Turkmenistan—there is an explicit limit on government involvement in the law. In the remaining countries, limits on direct credit to the government are incorporated in the annual fiscal budget to be adopted by the legislature.[9]

A central bank must be financially sound to remain autonomous. Lack of financial resources can influence the central bank to pursue policies contradictory with its objective(s). Thus it is important that only realized profits be transferred to the budget, and separate revaluation accounts should be created for nonrealized valuation gains and losses. The central banks in the 15 countries generally have sound provisions in place requir-

[8]The term varies from four to nine years in the 15 countries: four years in Russia; five years in Armenia, Azerbaijan, and Estonia; six years in Latvia; seven years in Georgia, the Kyrgyz Republic, Moldova, and Turkmenistan; and nine years in Lithuania. (Terms are staggered in Armenia, the Kyrgyz Republic, and Lithuania.) In Kazakhstan, the external members are appointed for the period of their office (i.e., a representative from the Supreme Council and the president, respectively, and two representatives from the Cabinet). However, in Belarus (ex officio members apparently for the period of their office), Tajikistan, Ukraine, and Uzbekistan, the terms for board members are not specified.

[9]In some countries, the law distinctly prohibits the central bank from participating in the primary market for government securities, which is a sound approach. The central bank, however, could be allowed to submit noncompetitive bids in an effort to build up its portfolio of government securities for open market operations. All 15 countries, with the exception of Latvia and Ukraine, require securitization. In Latvia, the central bank rarely lends to the government, and it is against the sale of treasury bills or drawing down deposits. With the exception of Azerbaijan, Belarus, Latvia, Russia, and Ukraine, all other countries explicitly stipulate that advances to the government shall bear a market-related interest rate. Moreover, several countries have explicit provisions that prevent the central bank from being involved in quasi-fiscal activities and in activities other than those necessary for conducting its primary functions.

ing recapitalization of any deficiency of authorized capital. Ideally, such a recapitalization should take place through government transfers of interest-bearing securities to the central bank, which are to be redeemed by future central bank profits before profits can formally be transferred to the government. Interest payments will ensure the bank a flow of income. Some of the countries have such provisions in place (Armenia, Georgia, Kyrgyz Republic, Moldova, and Turkmenistan), while other countries do not explicitly specify that the securities shall be interest-bearing (Belarus and Tajikistan). In the remaining countries, losses that may deplete the authorized capital of the central bank will typically have to be covered by future profits of the bank.

To avoid undue influence by the government on the implementation of monetary policy, the central bank should not be subject to short-term appropriation procedures.[10] In most of the central banks of the countries reviewed, the board is responsible for approving the budget of the bank. In Armenia and Lithuania, however, the annual budget is subject to approval of the legislature.[11]

Accountability

The central bank should be accountable to the government, legislature, and the general public for both its monetary policy and its use of public funds. Depending on the institutional structure, most of the central banks in the Baltics, Russia, and other countries of the former Soviet Union are formally accountable to the president, the legislature, or both. The laws all have provisions that require the bank to make at least one published annual statement on monetary policy, although in some instances the statement is subject to government approval. Several laws require more frequently published statements, for instance, twice a year, or when a release of information of importance for monetary policy is deemed necessary by the central bank or is requested by the legislature (Armenia, Azerbaijan, Estonia, Kyrgyz Republic, Lithuania, Moldova, Russia, and Tajikistan).

Because central banks are responsible for public money, including the seignorage created by the issue of the currency, sound business practices are important to establish central bank credibility and to support its autonomy from the government. Provisions that provide for the appro-

[10]If a central bank believes that it is necessary for the government to monitor the bank, it should probably consider longer budget periods to avoid undue influence by the government, as is the policy in New Zealand.

[11]The law in Armenia states that the budget be sufficient to allow the bank to fulfill its objectives and responsibilities.

Table 7.2. Amendments of Banking Legislation
(Until the end of 1997)

Country	Amendments of Banking Legislation	Most Recent Current Amendment (Date of adoption)	Under Review
Armenia	1993	Fall 1996	Yes
Azerbaijan	1992	August 1996	No
Belarus	1990, 1991, 1992, 1993, and 1994	December 1994	Yes[1]
Estonia	1990 and 1991	December 1994	Yes[2]
Georgia	1991 and 1996	March 1996	No
Kazakhstan	1990, 1992, 1993, and 1995	July 1997	No
Kyrgyz Republic	1991 and 1992	July 1997	No
Latvia	1995	October 1995	Yes
Lithuania	1992, 1994, 1995, 1996, and 1997	December 1997	Yes
Moldova	1992	July 1997	No
Russia	1990, 1991, 1992, 1993, 1994, 1995, and 1996	September 1997	Yes
Tajikistan	1991 and 1993	1994	Yes
Turkmenistan	1992	October 1993	No
Ukraine	1991	January 1995	Yes
Uzbekistan	1991 and 1992	April 1996	No

Source: IMF staff.

[1]Draft banking code is currently being reviewed by the Budget and Finance Commission of the House of Representatives.

[2]Legislation being amended with a view to achieve consistency with the future European System of Central Banks.

priate governmental oversight of the central bank will thus add to the credibility of the central bank. Several countries' central bank laws already include a stipulation that financial statements conform to International Accounting Standards (Armenia, Moldova, Lithuania, and Tajikistan).

Commercial Bank and Other Legislation

The 15 countries under review have also achieved significant progress in adopting and amending commercial bank legislation in response to the developing needs of a market-oriented economy. In general, the countries have built a legal framework for licensing banks, issuing prudential regulations consistent with the standards of the Bank for International Settlements (BIS), providing authority to the banking supervisor to conduct on-site and off-site supervision, and allowing the banking supervisor to impose sanctions for noncompliance. Furthermore, in response to the widespread incidence of undercapitalized or insolvent banks, commercial bank legislation has also generally been amended to clarify the regulations for conservatorship, receivership, and liquidation. Since the breakup of the Soviet Union, all of the countries have amended their commercial bank legislation, but addressing shortcomings in the laws has been a continuous effort. Kazakhstan and the Kyrgyz Republic, for instance, adopted substantial amendments in 1997 to bring this legislation in line with modern practice, while other countries—for example, Belarus, Estonia, and Tajikistan—were expected to amend their commercial bank legislation in 1998 to further improve and clarify the legal framework (Table 7.2). Lithuania also introduced revised amendments in 1997.

As growth begins to accelerate and banks begin to diversify into other related activities, such as leasing companies, as already seen in some countries, there is a need to clarify the legislation on such activities. Higher priority must be given to consolidated supervision and coordination with supervisors of nonbank financial companies. In some countries, for example Azerbaijan, the existing legislation may mainly need to be redefined, while in other countries, new legislation may be required on the activities and supervision of nonbank financial institutions, for example, in Turkmenistan and Ukraine, which has already drafted a law on nonbank financial organizations. (For further details on banking supervision and commercial bank legislation, see Chapter 4.)

An appropriate general legislative framework is needed to ensure that commercial banks can make binding decisions with the knowledge that repayment schedules will be respected and that collateral pledges will be enforced. The countries under review have generally made significant headway in adjusting the legal framework to the needs of a market-oriented economy. These advances include basic laws governing property rights and contracts, bankruptcy, and the use of collateral, including registration of liens. The principal weaknesses are now found not in law, although much remains to be done, but rather in the infrastructure required for the administration and enforcement of existing laws to meet the needs of a market-oriented economy.[12] In particular, the civil code has been amended to include property rights and contractual law, which better allows for the use of decentralized information, and facilitates debt repayment by individuals and business enterprises. Some countries, including Belarus, Tajikistan, Turkmenistan, and Ukraine, are currently working on additional amendments, while others, for example, Armenia and Azerbaijan, have identified shortcomings or are planning to amend the civil code to further ensure an appropriate legal framework. Although

[12]Moreover, about half of the countries in transition have already adopted or are currently preparing legal provisions against money laundering.

Table 7.3. Progress on Central Bank Legislation

I Limited Progress	II Moderate Progress	III Substantial Progress
Belarus, 1995[1]	Azerbaijan, 1996	Armenia, 1996
Ukraine, 1991[1]	Kazakhstan, 1997	Estonia, 1994[1]
	Latvia, 1992[1]	Georgia, 1995
	Russia, 1995	Kyrgyz Republic, 1997
	Tajikistan, 1996	Lithuania, 1997[1]
	Turkmenistan, 1993	Moldova, 1995
	Uzbekistan, 1995	

Note: The year represents the most recent amendment of the central bank law until the end of 1997.
[1]Indicates that the law is currently under review.

land ownership or land use is generally accepted, there may still remain judicial and practical impediments for using land as collateral, as in the Kyrgyz Republic.

Country Rankings

Rankings have only been assigned for central banking legislation (see Table 7.3).[13] A ranking for banking supervision can be found in Chapter 4. Rankings have been assigned on the basis of a comparison of the provisions in the four key areas described earlier with those of the guidelines discussed above. Six countries have adopted central bank laws broadly consistent with all four criteria, and have been assigned a ranking of substantial progress (Group III). Most of the other countries have also made considerable progress in adopting central bank autonomy, but provisions could be strengthened further with the result that these countries have accordingly been assigned the ranking of moderate progress (Group II). In this group, Kazakhstan, Latvia, Russia, and Uzbekistan have made the most notable progress. In Kazakhstan, provisions against arbitrary dismissal of members of the governing bodies could be improved, and the government should be explicitly obliged to recapitalize the bank by transferring interest-bearing securities in case of depletion of its authorized capital. Russia should place explicit limits on direct credit to the federal government, prohibit quasi-fiscal activities introduced by other legislation, and pass an explicit provision to recapitalize the bank in case of significant losses instead of using future profits. In Uzbekistan, the term and

[13]Advice has been provided by both the IMF's Monetary and Exchange Affairs and Legal Departments.

dismissal conditions for board members, with the exception of the governor, are not explicit, and there is no explicit limit on direct credit to the government.

Two countries have made limited progress, but they appear to be headed in opposite directions. In Ukraine, the legislature is currently discussing amendments that will significantly improve the autonomy of the central bank. In Belarus, however, the amendments presently being discussed will profoundly reduce the autonomy of the central bank.

Priorities for Reform

Central bank legislation that does not yet fully conform with the four criteria of price stability, political autonomy, economic autonomy, and accountability should be amended accordingly. Two considerations are particularly important—a rigorous limit on direct credit to the government and strict avoidance of all quasi-fiscal activities. Moreover, to gain actual legal autonomy and achieve price stability, the objectives and functions of the central bank must be explained to the general public.

Price stability reduces some of the uncertainties that confront financial intermediaries and the real sector, but with the stabilization of the economies, the shortcomings of the legal systems in these countries have become more visible. For a market economy to function properly, the government must ensure that generally accepted and transparent rules, clearly defined contractual rights, procedures for resolution of disputes over contracts, and the enforcement of all of the above must be credible and predictable. The introduction of generally accepted accounting principles, disclosure requirements, and the establishment of a core of independent external auditors will also contribute to a consistent flow of reliable information, and thus will also help to reduce uncertainty and facilitate a more efficient resource allocation. The Baltics, Russia, and other countries of the former Soviet Union have made considerable progress in establishing an appropriate legal framework, but reform is an ongoing process, and shortcomings must be addressed continuously. Priority must also be given to enforcing the existing legislation in a predictable way. The legal framework and the government's policies must be cohesive and create sound incentives that will promote an efficient resource allocation.

8

Background Tables

The following tables provide a summary of the reforms in the key central banking areas for the Baltics, Russia, and other countries of the former Soviet Union. The tables start with the implementation of monetary policy—specifically, the institutional context in which the central bank operates and its short- and medium-term operating targets, markets and interest rate management, and instruments and operating arrangements. They then move on to developments in the foreign exchange area and priorities for future reform. Significant attention is devoted to banking supervision and bank restructuring—first, the institutional framework of the banking system is covered; then, the structure and performance of the banking system is summarized; and, finally, bank restructuring measures in the individual countries are listed. The chapter concludes with summaries of payment systems and central bank accounting reforms.

Table 8.1. Institutional Background for Monetary Policy Implementation, 1997

	Central Bank Autonomy	Medium-Term Operating Framework and Targets	Short-Term Operating Framework and Targets
Armenia	A revised central bank law was adopted in June 1996, giving more autonomy to the central bank while increasing accountability. The draft law states that the prime objective of the central bank is the achievement of price stability.	The central bank uses broad money as intermediate target. Monetary performance criteria under the program supported by the IMF include a ceiling on net domestic assets (NDA) of the central bank and a floor for net international reserves (NIR) of the central bank, with an indicative target for broad money.	The monetary base is used as the operating target. Interest rates from deposit and treasury bill auctions are used as indicators. Levels of the central bank's NIR and NDA are very closely monitored. Foreign exchange intervention is used only to smooth sharp changes in the exchange rate or as a monetary instrument, with the exchange rate allowed to move more freely from late 1996.
Azerbaijan	A new central bank law was passed in June 1996. The law contains two key elements: (1) the central bank must maintain price stability and develop and strengthen the banking system; and (2) the Azerbaijan National Bank has independence to operate monetary and exchange rate policy. The law specifies that the central bank reports only to the president of the Azerbaijan Republic, and its financing of the government is limited to an amount that is determined by the National Assembly.	Monetary performance criteria under the program supported by the IMF include a ceiling on NDA of the central bank and a floor for the NIR of the central bank (on all currencies and on convertible currencies), with an indicative target for reserve money in manats.	The central bank has been giving an increasing weight to adhering to a reserve money target. Up-to-date banking figures are readily available, including the central bank's daily balance sheet. The authorities have a good general awareness of targets to be monitored under the program supported by the IMF. However, as the central bank moves toward more sophisticated and frequent monetary operations, it may need a stronger capacity for short-term forecasting of financial flows. In addition, the collection and monitoring of market information will need to keep pace with the expansion of markets.

Belarus	The National Bank of Belarus appears to have lost the limited autonomy it had following the referendum on constitutional reform. Monetary and exchange rate policies are determined by the government and the central bank. The bank's governor is a member of the cabinet of ministers but does not have ministerial rank.	There is no program supported by the IMF. Each quarter the central bank establishes maximum conditions for the bank's net ruble internal credit.	Liquidity forecasts are systematically made on a daily basis for the next two weeks. Banks' reserves are the day-to-day operating target.
Estonia	Central bank autonomy is not applicable because there is a currency board arrangement. The Bank of Estonia does not lend to the government.	Estonia has a program supported by a precautionary Stand-By Arrangement from the IMF. Under the performance criteria of the arrangement, the currency board's kroon liabilities are to be fully backed with foreign exchange at all times.	The central bank is bound by a money-creation rule that limits growth in base money to the growth in foreign exchange reserves. There is a fixed exchange rate. The central bank has not been managing the liquidity of the banking system actively.
Georgia	Objectives of the central bank are to maintain price stability and to foster the liquidity, solvency, and proper functioning of a stable market-based financial system. A new law enhancing the independence of the central bank was enacted in mid-1995. After operating for a prolonged period under an acting president, a new president of the central bank was confirmed by parliament on March 20, 1998.	Monetary performance criteria under the program supported by the IMF include a ceiling on NDA of the National Bank of Georgia and a floor on its NIR, with a financial benchmark for reserve money (including currency issued, required reserves, and balances in correspondent accounts).	Exchange rate developments are strongly influenced by the central bank's interventions in the foreign exchange market. Significant progress has been made in establishing a liquidity management framework. However, difficulties prevail in projecting government transactions.

Table 8.1 ***(continued)***

	Central Bank Autonomy	Medium-Term Operating Framework and Targets	Short-Term Operating Framework and Targets
Kazakhstan	Under the 1995 central bank law, the National Bank of Kazakhstan has considerable autonomy in implementing monetary policy. The central bank's objective is to maintain internal and external stability of the national currency. Beginning in January 1998, the National Bank will cease to grant credit to the government to finance budget deficits.	Monetary performance criteria under the program supported by the IMF include a ceiling for the central bank's NDA, a floor for its NIR, and an indicative target for base money.	The Technical Committee of Monetary and Exchange Rate Policy (established in August 1995, and whose composition changed in May 1996) meets weekly to assess developments in the exchange rate, international reserves, central bank credit, and base money. The committee continuously monitors compliance with monthly targets, which are derived from quarterly targets formulated with the IMF. Liquidity projections are complicated by difficulties in gathering information on government transactions.
Kyrgyz Republic	The law, adopted in 1992, established a relatively high degree of autonomy for the National Bank of the Kyrgyz Republic. A new law, passed in 1997, prohibits direct lending to the government after January 1998, as well as direct participation in the primary auction of government debt. The law also contains provisions to enhance the transparency of central bank operations, regulates its relations with the government and other financial institutions, and defines the bank's responsibility for currency policy.	Monetary performance criteria under the program supported by the IMF include ceilings on the central bank's NDA and the banking system's net claims on government, as well as a floor on NIR. Indicative targets include reserve money and NDA of the banking system.	Quarterly forecasts are based on extrapolations for the central bank's main balance sheet items, split into monthly figures. Day-to-day monetary operations keep a close watch on reserve money and central bank credit to the government, in addition to keeping track of the foreign exchange, treasury bill, and credit markets.

Latvia	The Bank of Latvia has a large degree of autonomy.	Monetary performance criteria under the program supported by the IMF include a ceiling on the central bank's NDA and a floor on its NIR, with an indicative target for reserve money and for the NDA of the banking system.	The central bank is building a database of daily figures, which are used for monitoring progress under the monetary program. Difficulties in forecasting the government's cash flows (in part because it holds accounts in several banks) and lack of coordination between monetary and foreign exchange operations make active liquidity management difficult.
Lithuania	Since April 1994, Lithuania has had a currency board arrangement. The authorities are considering replacing the currency board, and adopting a new law ensuring the autonomy and accountability of the Bank of Lithuania. The Bank of Lithuania does not lend to the government.	Currency board liabilities (reserve money and other liabilities denominated by litas) are to be fully backed with foreign exchange at all times. In addition, the exchange rate is fixed.	The central bank is bound by a money-creation rule that limits growth in base money to the growth in foreign exchange reserves at the fixed exchange rate. The central bank generates limited amounts of reserve money through loans on open market operations, which may not exceed the established level of free foreign reserves.
Moldova	The objective of the central bank is to maintain stability of the national currency. The National Bank of Moldova (NBM) has independence to operate monetary and exchange rate policies. The central bank's administrative council, in consultation with the government (primarily the Ministry of Finance), adopts an annual monetary program that is communicated to parliament every February.	Monetary performance criteria under the program supported by the IMF include ceilings on the central bank's NDA and net claims in the government and a floor for the bank's net international reserves in hard currencies, with indicative targets for the bank's gross international reserves, reserve money, and broad money.	Since November 1995, the NBM has used reserve money as its main monetary target. The reserve money target, and its associated NDA and net foreign asset (NFA) levels, are usually adjusted based on the quarterly program targets. The short-term liquidity forecasting capacity, however, needs strengthening.

Table 8.1 ***(continued)***

	Central Bank Autonomy	Medium-Term Operating Framework and Targets	Short-Term Operating Framework and Targets
Russia	The central bank law passed in 1995 enhanced the independence of the Central Bank of Russia.	Monetary performance criteria for 1997 include a ceiling on the central bank's NDA, defined as currency plus required reserves of commercial banks minus the NIR of the monetary authorities (central bank, government, and the Vneshekonombank). In addition, there is a floor for NIR of the monetary authorities. The program with the IMF includes quarterly performance criteria.	*Liquidity forecasting:* A five-day reporting system, introduced in 1995, allows the central bank to monitor banks' liquidity. Information on domestic and foreign currency developments is incorporated in the five-day reporting system. Treasury bill yields, the interbank market rate, and the exchange rate are used to guide monetary policy. There is still a need for improved coordination between the money and foreign exchange desks. The central bank pursues an interest rate objective that is subsidiary to the exchange rate.
Tajikistan	A new law that substantially enhances the National Bank of Tajikistan's (NBT) autonomy was adopted in December 1996.	Monetary targets include a ceiling for the central bank's NDA and a floor for its net international reserves.	Short-term operating targets are set in line with the monetary program formulated with the IMF. The central bank's foreign exchange operations have been used to manage short-term liquidity. While the central bank performs some liquidity forecasting, its framework needs to be strengthened, particularly operational data on state revenues and expenses received during each month, and on adjustments of the balances of the treasury's current account.

Turkmenistan	In the past, the Central Bank of Turkmenistan has had little autonomy in the conduct of monetary policy, with decisions on the quantity and cost of central bank credit generally taken by the government and enforced by presidential decree. A reform program announced in late 1995 gave the central bank more autonomy in principle to implement a monetary policy aimed at price stability. Directed credits by presidential decree at highly negative real interest rates have been repeated in 1997. In addition, a presidential decree gave the central bank responsibility for preparing and implementing Turkmenistan's annual monetary and foreign exchange program, which in practice meant fashioning a program to compensate for the monetary expansion resulting from a substantial amount of subsidized agricultural credit. At the same time, by mid-year the central bank was obliged to provide credit to wheat growers at zero interest rates.	There is no program supported by the IMF. The progress in monetary programming has been slow, reflecting the difficulty in projecting various balance sheet items, the existence of large quantities of quasi- and off-budget expenditures, and the lack of coordination with the Ministry of Economy and Finance.	The central bank uses projections prepared by the IMF as basis for setting liquidity targets, but the development of market-based interest rates has been hampered by the discontinuation of the credit auctions in March 1997.
Ukraine	Current (1991) legislation establishes some autonomy for the National Bank of Ukraine. The latest draft Law on the National Bank of Ukraine, which provides for effective independence, was considered on first reading in parliament in October 1997.	Monetary performance criteria under the program supported by the IMF include a ceiling on central bank NDA and a floor for NIR, with an indicative target for reserve money.	Within the medium-term framework, interest rates are the main operating target. Substantial progress has been made in developing a monitoring framework for short-term money and exchange market conditions, as well as a reporting framework for key program variables. Short-term forecasts of commercial banks' reserves are prepared by the central bank.

Table 8.1 ***(concluded)***

	Central Bank Autonomy	Medium-Term Operating Framework and Targets	Short-Term Operating Framework and Targets
Uzbekistan	The central bank law passed in 1995 enhanced the independence of the central bank, whose main objective is to maintain price stability. The central bank has independence to operate monetary and exchange rate policy. However, no formal limit is set on central bank financing of the government; central bank credit extended to the government must be approved by parliament.	There is no program supported by the IMF.	The central bank monitors commercial bank correspondent account balances closely. Basic operating targets are reserve money and excess reserves of commercial banks. The bank is developing an operating system to monitor banking system liquidity and reserve money changes.

Sources: Country authorities; and IMF.

Table 8.2. Markets and Interest Rate Management, 1997

	Interbank Market	Government Securities Market	Interest Rate Management
Armenia	The interbank market has operated freely since July 1995. Trading has been limited in part because of risks in lending to banks and the absence of collateral in some banks (although these factors should be less important in the future), in addition to a general lack of pressure on excess bank reserves.	*Primary market:* Auctioning of treasury bills with maturities of up to one year started in September 1995, with preannounced minimum price and uniform price determination. The Ministry of Finance decides on timing, amount, and cutoff price. Outstanding volumes have continued to grow (by over 30 percent of M2 as of the end of 1997), partly based on demand from offshore sources. Auction participation has been growing, but often the auctions have not been fully covered by a price/yield deemed "reasonable" by the government, in which case the government uses its right to cut off the tender amount. However, this generally occurs less frequently than in the past. *Secondary market:* Virtually nonexistent due in part to a tax distortion, but this has recently been removed.	Deposit and lending rates of commercial banks are market-determined. The refinance rate set by the Central Bank of Armenia (positive in real terms throughout 1996) is used for setting the interest rate on central bank loans to government and the Lombard rate.
Azerbaijan	Most commercial banks redeposit their clients' foreign currency deposits in one commercial bank (the Azerbaijan International Bank); some interbank deposits in manat occur on an interbank over-the-counter (OTC) (unorganized) interbank market; and commercial banks are allowed to offer refinance credit at the credit auction, but in practice only the central bank offers credit.	*Primary market:* Regular monthly auctions of one-month treasury bills commenced in September 1996. Three-month bills are already being offered, and six-month bills are envisaged for the near future. Twenty-three banks have been selected as primary dealers. The market is still very thin. *Secondary market:* In place, but trading is weak due to the small volume in circulation and the short maturity of the bills.	Deposit and lending rates of commercial banks are market-determined. Rates vary widely according to banks and client groups, reflecting a highly segmented financial market that lacks efficient arbitrage. The refinance rate since March 1995 has been determined at the credit auction.

Table 8.2 *(continued)*

	Interbank Market	Government Securities Market	Interest Rate Management
Belarus	The interbank market developed steadily throughout 1995, becoming volatile toward the end of the year, as a result of the transfer of government and state-enterprise deposits to a newly merged bank. The market remained periodically volatile in 1996, mostly due to large injections of liquidity by the National Bank of Belarus (NBB) through directed credits. Volume grew over the course of 1997, while yields declined. Mid-month instability was partly due to seasonal fluctuations linked to tax payments. Central bank liquidity management operations had a stabilizing effect on the market.	*Primary market:* A market involving auctioning of treasury bills started in 1994 using the multiple price auction. Volumes have been growing; maturities of bills are from 6 to 12 months (as compared to one to six months in 1996). Auctions of long-term bonds have been held since October 1997. In both cases, the Ministry of Finance (MOF) decides on timing, maturity, amount, and the cutoff price. *Secondary market:* Consisting of banks and other financial institutions, this market has continued to grow. The market is expected to be structured as an exchange. Individuals are not allowed to operate in the treasury bill and long-term bond market.	The lending rates are market-determined, with the exception of loans issued within the framework of state programs, on which interest rates and margins are regulated by the government. *Deposit rates:* The minimum rate on deposits was eliminated in 1995 and reinstated in March 1997. *Refinance rate:* This rate is set by the National Bank and adjusted regularly with a view to keeping it above the anticipated rate of inflation. The refinance rate has been negative during most of 1997. The rate is used to finance the budget deficit and as a reference rate for nontargeted bank refinancing through repo and swap operations. Aside from the refinance rate, since October 1997 the central bank holds auctions of collateral credit, in which a fixed pre-set collateral rate is used as the minimum rate when submitting bids. Rates on banks' deposits with the central bank are also used to set a floor for the interbank interest rate.
Estonia	The interbank market is used by commercial banks to minimize excess reserves. The variability of	There is no treasury bill market.	Deposit and lending rates of commercial banks are market-determined. Until November 1997, interest rates corresponded

	interest rates was low during the first half of 1997, increasing in the third quarter. Bank of Estonia certificates of deposit may be used as collateral in interbank operations; certificates of deposit were issued for market development purposes. In 1997, the role of the interbank market in bank liquidity management diminished, and activity was especially low in the fourth quarter. Transactions with maturities longer than one week have been rare.		closely to German interest rates. The rise in base interest rates in mid-November 1997 reflects changes in the money market as well as measures taken by the central bank to tighten monetary conditions. The Bank of Estonia certificate of deposit rate has generally tracked the deutsche mark interbank market rate. The actual rate, however, is determined in monthly auctions. The interbank market rate, previously close to the short end (overnight to one week) of the deutsche mark interbank market rate, has risen sharply since September 1997 because of a temporary liquidity squeeze in the banking sector, determined by the substantial lending activity in the first half of 1997 and by the events in international money and capital markets.
Georgia	Commercial banks are allowed to borrow and lend at the interbank credit auction. While still somewhat thin, activity in the interbank credit market has picked up in 1997.	Auctions of treasury bills started in August 1997. The primary market is still very thin and the secondary market is virtually nonexistent.	Deposit and lending rates of commercial banks are market-determined. Although interest rates are positive in real terms, deposit mobilization remains low due to the lack of confidence in the banking system. Prudential limits on mobilization of household deposits were liberalized in January 1997; the limits on such deposits were increased from the amount of a bank's capital to nine times the amount. *Refinance rate:* A Lombard facility was introduced in August 1997 with the rate set at a premium over the 28-day treasury bill rate.

Table 8.2 *(continued)*

	Interbank Market	Government Securities Market	Interest Rate Management
Kazakhstan	The short-term money market was established in April 1995 with participation of the Central Clearing House, the National Bank of Kazakhstan, and 11 banks licensed by the central bank. Maturities of 1–30 days are traded. Collateral may be required for transactions of more than 14 days. Settlement takes place on the central bank books. The number of participants and the daily turnover increased until December 1995, but the turnover fell sharply in 1996, reflecting concern about the health of the financial system. At present transactions are conducted almost exclusively in the off-exchange interbank market.	*Primary market:* The first auction of three-month treasury bills took place in April 1994. With declining inflation, maturity of treasury bills was extended to six months in July 1995, and 12 months in July 1996. Stocks have been growing steadily at declining yields. In 1997, two-year bonds were introduced in auction format. One-year government bonds have been in circulation since 1996. Government securities are primarily issued for financing the budget deficit. *Secondary market* (OTC): Trading has expanded. A comprehensive regulatory framework for secondary operations, including repurchase agreements and electronic delivery-versus-payment settlement, was introduced by mid-1996. The market conducts repurchase and reverse repurchase operations. To manage liquidity, the central bank has recently begun repo operations in limited volumes.	Deposit and lending rates of commercial banks are market-determined. Bank margins are high, reflecting the high level of nonperforming loans. The refinance rate, which is charged on lending to the government, is set by the central bank. It is adjusted regularly in line with inflation to keep it positive in real terms and in accordance with the state of financial markets

Kyrgyz Republic	The over-the-counter (OTC) interbank market operates freely, and the volume is growing.	*Primary market:* Weekly multiple rate auctions of three- and six-month and one-year treasury bills are held. Primary dealership was established in 1996 and currently comprises 13 commercial banks. Since July 1997, large companies and nonprimary dealer banks may participate directly in the auction. An electronic trading system for government securities that links primary dealers with market participants was implemented in April 1998. A one-year non-negotiable savings bond with a flexible rate linked to the central bank's refinance rate may be issued in 1998. *Secondary market:* An electronic trading system for government securities that links primary dealers with market participants will start to operate in 1998.	Deposit and lending rates of commercial banks are market-determined. The refinance rate (Lombard) is linked to the 90-day treasury bill rate.
Latvia	The interbank market operates freely. Maturities traded vary from overnight to between three months and one year. The market remains thin and interest rates relatively volatile. Rates on foreign currency-denominated transactions have fallen to levels that are only just above foreign rates (as proxied by the SDR interest rate). Rates on domestic currency-denominated transactions have fallen below the Bank of Latvia refinance rate.	*Primary market:* Auctions of treasury bills were introduced in December 1993 (multiple-price auction). Now 28-day, 91-day, 182-day, and one-year bills are offered in weekly auctions. Two-year bills were introduced in April 1997. *Secondary market*: Few banks are active in this market, and the amounts traded are small. A secondary window, which was established by the central bank in April 1994, provided substantial liquidity to the market.	Deposit and lending rates of commercial banks are market-determined. The refinance rate is the central bank's core interest rate, which is used to determine the rate on repurchase operations and the rates at the Lombard window.

Table 8.2 *(continued)*

	Interbank Market	Government Securities Market	Interest Rate Management
Lithuania	The interbank market operates freely. It has been relatively inactive since the beginning of 1996 because of the banking crisis, but has recently begun to increase again. There is a small amount of interbank activity with treasury bills used as collateral among three or four banks.	*Primary market:* Multiple-price treasury bill auctions, which were introduced in 1994, have been held since then. One-, three-, and six-month and one-year bills are offered in weekly auctions. No cutoff rate is set prior to the auction. *Secondary market:* The stock exchange organizes trading sessions daily. Commissions were lowered in October 1997. The savings bank holds more than half of the outstanding treasury bills and could become a market-maker. Limiting factors are the lack of trading skills and absence of an electronic information system linking market participants. The new Regulations for Government Securities Markets, recently adopted, introduced the OTC secondary market for treasury bills.	Deposit and lending rates of commercial banks are market-determined. Interest rates declined dramatically following the establishment of the currency board arrangement and currently are close to international rates. *Emergency lending rate:* The Bank of Lithuania announces official lending rates for liquidity and overnight loans.

Moldova	In the year ended October 1997, the volume of transactions in the OTC interbank market (primarily one- to three-month loans) increased 420 percent. Government securities are used as collateral.	*Primary market:* Auctions of 91-day treasury bills were introduced in March 1995; the range of maturity on offer has been expanded from durations of 28 and 91 days to 182, 273, 364 days, and two years. Special-purpose bonds are also issued with a maturity of 365 days and a fixed coupon rate. The Ministry of Finance published a three-month schedule of auctions indicating the amount of securities to be offered at each auction; sales are to banks approved as primary dealers. Sales based on individual contracts were seen as undermining the auction process and were therefore eliminated in January 1997. An electronic book-entry system was implemented in February 1996 by the National Bank of Moldova. A 15 percent 365-day discount bond was introduced in December 1996 (effectively paying 33 percent), and a two-year fixed rate bond with a coupon rate of 15 percent was issued at the end of 1997. *Secondary market:* Trading is beginning to get under way. An electronic data-processing system linking primary dealers and market participants is expected to be introduced in early 1998. A 0.3 percent tax on secondary transactions had been charged to the purchaser, limiting market development; this tax was canceled effective January 1, 1998.	Deposit and lending rates of commercial banks are market-determined. In February 1994, the central bank eliminated all remaining limits on interest rate margins applied to central bank credit on-lent to commercial banks, with the exception of loans guaranteed by the government. Refinance rate has been established by credit auctions since November 1993.

Table 8.2 *(continued)*

	Interbank Market	Government Securities Market	Interest Rate Management
Russia	Markets were active in both rubles and foreign exchange until the August 1995 interbank market crisis. Market segmentation impedes the arbitrage within regions and markets. Core activity is at money center banks or clearing banks and at financial organizations owned by commercial banks. Maturities of ruble deposits and loans are largely of one to seven days, and most credit is unsecured. Lack of settlement balance account information may be hampering market development. On February 28, 1997, the Central Bank of Russia (CBR) introduced a multiple-clearing system (four sessions).	*Primary market:* A market in treasury bills (GKOs) of maturities up to one year has been ongoing since May 1993. GKOs are auctioned mainly for domestic debt management purposes. In 1995 a new instrument, the federal loan bond with a variable interest coupon (OFZ-PK), was introduced, with a maturity of longer than one year, and with the interest rate coupon linked to the yield on three-month GKOs. In December 1996, an OFZ-PK with a six-month maturity was introduced. Federal loan bonds with a fixed coupon yield (OFZ-PDs) with a maturity of up to 8 years have been on the market since 1997. There was a 25% rate of growth in volumes of primary placement in 1997 compared with 1996. *Secondary market:* A computer-based market administered by the Moscow Interbank Currency Exchange (MICEX) is rapidly growing. GKOs and OFZs are traded four times a week in 2½ hour trading sessions; all bonds are held in electronic book-entry form at MICEX, where regional trading began in 1996, with banks and financial companies outside Moscow having online access; transaction prices are rigidly pegged to the current MICEX situation, and the transactions themselves are registered with MICEX.	Deposit and lending rates of commercial banks are market-determined. The refinance rate is set in relation to the GKO market yield and the inflation rate. It is only used to set the overdraft facility rate and as a basis for rates for one-day settlement credits. The repo rate is the rate at which primary dealers in the government securities market borrow from the central bank to cover overnight shortfalls related to securities trading. A two-session mechanism for effecting repo operations was introduced in September 1997. The rate of the first session is determined from results of bidding at the primary dealer auction, and the rate of the second session is fixed and established by the central bank at a higher level. From February 1998, the Lombard rate has been established for 3–7, 8–14, and 15–30-day collateralized credit. Since November 1997 deposit rates have been established daily for ruble funds attracted by commercial banks for one day on an "overnight" or "tomnext" basis, and for seven days. Yields on treasury bills are market-determined, although the Ministry of Finance

		A system of primary dealers was established (at the end of 1997 there were 37) who can operate with a short cash position limit. The central bank holds two daily repo sessions: the first one in the morning in a primary dealer auction format; the second one at a higher fixed rate for primary dealers who need to cover overnight short positions.	and the central bank sometimes intervene to smooth market fluctuations.
Tajikistan	The interbank money market is still at an embryonic stage of development. An interbank credit auction market was established in May 1995 to facilitate interbank transactions, but auctions were halted in August 1995. Limited over-the-counter trading among banks is taking place.	There is no market for government securities as yet. Primary auctions of treasury bills are scheduled to commence in the second half of 1998.	Deposit and lending rates of commercial banks are market-determined (the 10 percent maximum margin between banks' lending rates and cost of funds was eliminated in 1995). Interest rates are positive in real terms. The central bank sets the refinance rate at the interest rate set at the credit auction plus 0.5 percent per month.
Turkmenistan	Commercial banks are allowed to borrow and lend freely among themselves, with some activity emerging, although the market remains thin and transactions are irregular, despite improvements in the timeliness of settlement balance account information. High-value transfers are handled separately, and some banks have electronic links to their branch network outside the capital. Interbank loans are unsecured and at positive real rates of interest. Interbank credit auctions are not active.	*Primary market:* Relatively small amounts have been issued since July 1994 (manat 8 billion by the end of 1997) at rates set by the Ministry of Economy and Finance; nonnegotiable; maturity was reduced from three months to one; issued in book-entry form; bought by commercial banks; with the exception of one auction in August 1996, the Ministry of Economy and Finance has acted independently from the central bank when issuing the treasury bills. *Secondary market:* Virtually nonexistent.	Deposit and lending rates of commercial banks, with the exception of a large volume of subsidized credit to key sectors, are market-determined and currently positive in real terms. A ceiling of 15 percent on commercial bank loans to state enterprises was eliminated in late 1995. The refinance rate since 1996 has been set in the central bank credit auctions, but now is directly set by the central bank with a view on developments in the inflation rate. In the first ten months of 1997, the refinance rate has declined from 105 percent to 35 percent while remaining positive in real terms.

Table 8.2 *(concluded)*

	Interbank Market	Government Securities Market	Interest Rate Management
Turkmenistan *(continued)*			*Directed credit:* Although in principle discontinued, a significant volume of directed credits were issued in December 1996 and mid-1997; interest rates on directed credits are set by presidential decree.
Ukraine	The interbank money market is active, although during 1996 the authorities intervened in order to direct lending to commercial banks with liquidity problems.	*Primary market:* The market continued to develop in 1997. Multiple-price auctions have been held daily since November 1997 (as compared to weekly by the end of 1996) and maturities offered regularly have been extended to include 546-day discount bonds. A total of 7.5 billion hryvnias worth of government securities was in circulation as of November 1997. The Ministry of Finance decides on timing, amount, and cutoff price after consultation with the National Bank of Ukraine, which is the government agent for auctions. The amounts of bills of each maturity to be offered for sale have been announced approximately one week in advance since January 1997. Significant nonresident purchases of treasury bills began in late 1996, with Ukrainian banks acting as agents for nonresident purchasers as required under law. Demand by nonresidents fell sharply in the last quarter of 1997. The government securities market operates on an electronic basis. *Secondary market:* Remains very thin. The central bank registers all secondary market transactions.	Deposit and lending rates of commercial banks are market-determined. The required link between lending rates and the refinance rate, which was introduced by the central bank in 1995, was abolished in late 1996. The refinance rate is set by the central bank and adjusted in line with inflation developments—normally positive in real terms.

Uzbekistan	Commercial banks are allowed to borrow and lend at credit auctions, but most credit is provided by the Central Bank of Uzbekistan.	*Primary market:* The first issue of treasury bills (GKO) occurred in March 1996, and the market is developing well. The volume of bills in circulation as of the end of October 1997 was 24.6 billion sum. Maturities are three and six months. *Secondary market:* Trades daily through a double auction, based on a trading system recently put in place. Turnover in secondary trading as of April 1, 1998 was 48.9 billion sum. Beginning in January 1998, nine primary dealers were selected as market-makers in bills, out of 22 dealers on the GKO market. The central bank conducts repurchase operations with primary dealers on the secondary market.	Deposit and lending rates of commercial banks are market-determined. The refinance rate is adjusted in line with inflation and market developments.

Sources: Country authorities; and IMF.

Table 8.3. Instruments and Operating Arrangements, 1997

	Reserve Requirements	Standing & Nonmarket-Based Discretionary Facilities	Market Operations	Other Instruments
Armenia	Differentiated reserve requirements by maturity were introduced in May 1996. Unified reserve requirements at 8 percent were introduced by decree in early January 1997 to take effect from August 1997. From June 1997, cash in banks' vaults will be excluded from the reserve requirement calculation. Since August 1997, at least 50 percent of the requirement on foreign-denominated deposits must be met in foreign currency whereas before, the requirement was up to 100 percent. Reserve balances are averaged over a two-week period, with a one-day lag.	*Overdraft facility:* No longer operational. *Directed credit:* Abolished in early 1995. *Lombard facility:* Credit provided for up to seven days, with a penalty interest rate of 1.3 times the refinance rate. *Systemic credit:* Uncollateralized credit is granted for up to one year, at somewhat concessional rates currently (inflation plus 20 percent). At least 30 percent of funds must be allocated to government securities, and 50 percent in interbank loans and commercial bank deposits.	*Credit auction:* No longer operational. *Central bank auctioned deposits:* Short-term Central Bank of Armenia deposits, which initially had 14- and 28-day terms, were introduced in September 1996. Outside auctions as a form of standing facility were also available. The central bank initially capped interest rates in auctions at well below treasury bill rates, but in December 1996 allowed auction rates to rise substantially. *An auction of government securities* held off-balance sheet by the central bank as collateral of the government credit line was held during the summer of 1997. The central bank signed a contract with the government to securitize the credit line in early 1998. The off-balance sheet treasury bills were auctioned alongside normal new issue bills in the treasury bill auction. *Repos and reverse repos:* These instruments were introduced on a very small scale in March 1996; they were	*Central bank foreign exchange operations:* Interventions now solely in the interbank market. In 1996 and 1997, the central bank used foreign currency sales as a main domestic monetary policy instrument, rather than orienting toward an exchange rate target, as the exchange rate was allowed to float more freely.

			then reintroduced more actively in early 1998 using the treasury bonds acquired by the central bank in the securitization of credit to government.	
Azerbaijan	Reserve requirements were unified at 12 percent in February 1997 (up from 8 percent and 6 percent on manat and foreign exchange-denominated deposits, respectively). Banks must meet requirements on manat deposits in manats, and on foreign currency deposits in foreign currency. Requirements are calculated on the basis of daily average deposit balances. There is no averaging of reserve holdings.	*Overdraft facility:* In late 1994, all automatic overdraft facilities were abolished. There is no formal lender-of-last resort facility. The central bank has provided such credit on an ad hoc basis to state-owned banks. Banks may also acquire refinance credit at a credit auction if they comply with the conditions for participation.	*Credit auction:* Open outcry auctions are conducted at Baku Interbank Currency Exchange (BICEX). Only banks that meet prudential regulations are allowed to participate. Substantial improvement in information dissemination and transparency during 1997 may help develop auctions in the near future. Since 1997, all refinance credit has been allocated through credit auctions, whose frequency was increased to weekly in 1998. A new draft regulation contains provisions requiring partial collateralization. The supply of credit is adjusted dynamically as the auction proceeds, but amounts sold are usually consistent with the central bank's credit policies. Auctions are held bimonthly with maturities varying from 3 to 180 days, although, in practice, only 180-day credits have faced a significant demand.	Foreign exchange sales at the BICEX are also used as a monetary instrument.

Table 8.3 *(continued)*

	Reserve Requirements	Standing & Nonmarket-Based Discretionary Facilities	Market Operations	Other Instruments
Belarus	Differentiated ratios ranging from 5 percent to 21 percent (decreasing with the holding period) apply to domestic and foreign currency-denominated bank deposits of up to one year, and may be fulfilled in either currency. Ratios on deposits of up to 90 days were raised in May 1997, and again in September 1997, while deposits of more than one year were exempted in May 1997. If over 20 (30) percent of banks' resources, excluding those provided by the National Bank of Belarus, are placed in investment credits, the ratio on deposits of over one month are reduced by 25 (50) percent. Since September 1997, banks may meet a portion of the requirement by purchasing government securities at primary placement. There is no averaging of reserves. Only reserve requirements on domestic currency deposits are remunerated at 12 percent, (with the exception of the Belarusbank, for which reserve requirements on domestic currency deposits are remunerated at 50 percent of the	*Directed credit*: Was the main channel of bank refinancing in 1997. Subsidized rates below the National Bank of Belarus (NBB) refinance rate apply. *Overdraft facility:* Permitted for a certain number of banks; limits set quarterly. Penalty rate of 3 times the refinance rate. An overdraft may be permitted for no more than 2 consecutive days, after which the NBB can suspend operations on the correspondent account. Effective January 1, 1998 overdrafts on correspondent accounts are prohibited.	*Credit auction*: Credit auctions with government securities as collateral have been held since October 1997. The maturity of issued credits is 7–12 days. The central bank conducts auctions as needed. There were few auctions in 1996 and 1997 due to the emphasis on directed credit. *Central bank short-term obligations*: Short-term obligations are issued for banks through auctions and for central banks of foreign states without holding auctions. *Central bank bills:* The bank has auctioned its own bills since July 1997. Central bank bills are sold to banks on an individual basis. The interest rate is set by the central bank at the level of the base refinancing rate. *Banks' deposits with the NBB:* Various terms; liquidity management purpose. Deposits are accepted based on banks' applications. Interest rates are differentiated based on terms of the deposits. *Secondary market for treasury bills:* The central bank has been purchasing and selling treasury bills in growing amounts.	

	refinance rate, and on freely convertible currency at 50 percent of LIBOR).		Operations are conducted on the over-the-counter and exchange markets. Emphasis is on a shift of all operations to the exchange market. *Repo operations:* Conducted in significant amounts on an individual basis and an auction basis during periods of liquidity shortages. *Swap operations*: Conducted in significant amounts on an individual basis for purposes of supporting liquidity of banks.
Estonia	There is a uniform reserve ratio of 10 percent, including domestic, foreign currency deposits, non-resident deposits (but excluding credit from foreign banks), and securities (but excluding subordinated debt). Eligible assets include deposits at the Bank of Estonia (BOE) and vault cash (cash can be no more than 40 percent of required reserves). Reserves on foreign currency deposits are to be maintained in domestic currency. There is a four-week maintenance period, and reserves are based on the average of deposit liabilities on the 10th, 20th, and the end of the preceding month. Reserve holdings are averaged, with a penalty rate of 20 percent (15 percent until October 1997) a year on the	The extension of central bank credit to commercial banks is limited to a portion of the amount of foreign exchange reserves in excess of those needed to provide full backing of base money. In this context, the central bank has provided emergency credit to commercial banks. The central bank introduced deposits with the central bank in the second half of 1996. It pays the commercial banks a rate equal to the discount rate of the Deutsche Bundesbank, on deposits exceeding the reserve requirements, including the temporary additional requirement.	*Certificates of deposit:* Issued for market development, rather than monetary management, through monthly auctions with sealed bids. Interest rate commission sets upper and lower bounds on accepted bids and decides on volume offered, which is small. December 1996 and January 1997 auctions failed because of lack of interest on the part of the banks. Interest remained very low during 1997. *Secondary market:* For CDs exists through electronic trading on the BOE depository system, with same-day settlement. The central bank stands ready to enter into repos of CDs.

Table 8.3 *(continued)*

	Reserve Requirements	Standing & Nonmarket-Based Discretionary Facilities	Market Operations	Other Instruments
Estonia *(continued)*	deficiency. Banks must keep at least 40 percent (20 percent until October 1997) of required reserves balance daily or be subject to penalty. Only excess reserves are remunerated. To enhance liquidity buffers and support the reduction of credit growth in November 1997, the central bank introduced an additional requirement for banks' reserve holdings at the central bank through the establishment of a temporary compulsory monthly minimum on the banks' balances in excess of 3 percent over the reserve requirement base in December 1997. (Previously the rate was 2 percent).			
Georgia	The uniform reserve ratio was reduced to 12 percent from 15 percent in late August 1997. There was virtually full compliance in 1997; foreign currency reserves are being held in domestic currency. Reserves are not averaged, and balances may be used to collateralize borrowing at the auction. Reserves are unremunerated.	*Overdraft facility:* As of September 1994, banks' automatic access to overdrafts was eliminated. *Lombard facility:* Introduced in August 1997.	*(Interbank) credit auction:* Open outcry method used; National Bank of Georgia can exclude banks not in compliance with prudential regulations. Up to 90 percent of a bank's reserve requirement may be used to collateralize borrowing at the auction (an increase from 75 percent in June 1996); the scale of operations, while small, is increasing. The auction deals with multiple maturities; central bank intervention is designed mainly to foster the development	Since December 1994, the central bank has used *foreign exchange operations* to moderate the monetary impact of its lending to the government.

			of the interbank market rather than to attain monetary policy objectives, but the central bank has borrowed in the market to manage liquidity. *Primary market*: Issues of treasury bills began in August 1997.	
Kazakhstan	The uniform ratio on domestic and foreign exchange deposits has been gradually lowered to 10 percent effective October 1997. The portion due on foreign currency deposits may be held in foreign currency. Reserve holdings are averaged. Remuneration of required reserves was eliminated as of October 1997. A penalty rate for noncompliance defines the maximum interest rate in the interbank market. Eligible assets for required reserves include vault cash, which is not remunerated.	*Lombard facility:* Introduced in September 1995 with treasury bills as collateral. The interest rate is currently set at a margin over the market rate. The maturity of the loan must be within one month. The Lombard facility has been little used given the existence of alternate arrangements for liquidity support. *Overnight credit mechanism*: Created in March 1997 at a rate above that of the interbank market. *Extended credit:* The National Bank of Kazakhstan grants extended credit (more than one month) collateralized by government securities, foreign currency, or gold.	*Centralized credit auctions:* Significantly reduced in 1996. The regional credit auctions, introduced in June 1994, were phased out by January 1996. Central bank securities with a maturity between 7 and 90 days, which were first introduced in mid–1995, were used on an ad hoc basis in 1996 to absorb liquidity. *Primary market* for treasury bills is not used for monetary management. The Technical Committee of Monetary and Exchange Rate Policy meets every Friday morning to discuss recent developments, based on an information package. It makes recommendations for the coming week, which are presented to management Friday afternoon. Management then issues guidelines for the use of various instruments. The guidelines can be amended during the week as necessary. *Secondary market for treasury bills* has recently developed, with the NBK increasingly purchasing and selling, including through repurchase agreements and reverse repurchase agreements.	The central bank's *operations in foreign exchange and precious metals* have on several occasions been used as monetary instruments.

Table 8.3 *(continued)*

	Reserve Requirements	Standing & Nonmarket-Based Discretionary Facilities	Market Operations	Other Instruments
Kyrgyz Republic	The uniform ratio rate was increased to 15 percent in December 1996, then to 20 percent on January 1, 1997. This rate applies to banks' domestic and foreign currency-denominated deposit liabilities. The reserve requirement must be held in domestic currency, and since March 1995 banks have been able to use cash in vault to meet the requirement. Effective April 1997, foreign exchange cash in vault can no longer be counted toward meeting reserve requirements. The requirement is based on the monthly average of banks' deposits with monthly maintenance period on average. As of April 1997, differentiated remuneration rates are computed based on each bank's deposit rate, and penalties of 1.4 times the National Bank of the Kyrgyz Republic's average monthly refinance rate for the report month apply in case of noncompliance, which has declined to some extent in 1997 (20 cases in the period January–July 1997, some of which were granted waivers by the NB).	*Lombard facility*: Redesigned in January 1997 so that the collateral requirement is now 100 percent, up from 50 percent. Collateral can be in the form of three-month treasury bills, foreign exchange, or precious metals. Maturity of credit is from 7 to 14 days. Interest rates are currently 1.2 times the central bank's refinance rate. The facility has been used four times in the period January to July 1997. *Emergency credit facility:* Introduced in November 1994, but was phased out in late 1996 for problem banks.	*Credit auctions:* abolished in December 1996. *Primary market for treasury bills:* Until late 1994, treasury bills served purely for monetary purposes. Now auction volume and timing is determined by the Ministry of Finance based on recommendations by the central bank. Weekly auctions are held. *Secondary market:* Effective mid-1997, the central bank began conducting repos for liquidity management, securitized by government debt (usually six months maturities). Operations are carried out daily.	*The central bank's foreign exchange operations:* Since January 1, 1998 weekly auctions have been held. Foreign exchange operations are partly used as a monetary instrument.
Latvia	Since July 1993, a uniform reserve ratio of 8 percent applies to banks' domestic and foreign currency-denominated deposit liabilities of	*Lombard facility:* Requires treasury bills as collateral. Rates on this facility are set at margins above the refinance rate as	*Repo auctions:* Replaced short-term credit auctions. Repo auctions are held every day, offering 7-, 28-, and 90-day loans. Treasury-bills are used as collateral.	*Foreign exchange operations:* Have been the main monetary policy

the preceding month, measured as of balances on the 7th, 15th, and last day of the month. Since September 1994, banks have been allowed to hold a maximum of 50 percent of their required reserves in vault cash. The remainder is held in non-interest-earning deposits with averaging of reserves. All the reserves are held in domestic currency. In case of noncompliance, banks pay a penalty of two and a half times the deficiency.	follows: 3 percent for 1 to 7-day loans, 5 percent for 8 to 14-day loans, and 7 percent for 15 days or more. Notification to draw on this facility has to be made before noon at the latest on the day of the drawing. Most Bank of Latvia (BOL) credit is now in the form of repos, as rates on such credits are guided by treasury bill rates, while the refinance rate has been higher than treasury bill rates. *Automatic Lombard (overdraft) facility:* Introduced in 1995 to help banks cover end-of-day clearing imbalances, for which treasury bills are required as collateral. Credit is extended on an overnight basis to banks that have signed collateral agreements. Banks are allowed to borrow up to 80 percent of the value of the collateral. The interest rate is 3 percent above the refinance rate. *Automatic deposit facility:* Introduced in 1995 (one-month deposits at the central bank at a fixed rate). *Extraordinary financing facility:* Introduced in 1995 for banks in serious difficulties. The facility has no ceiling, and financing is provided for up to 30 days. No collateral is required.	*Treasury bill secondary window:* Established in 1994. The central bank quotes bid/offer prices daily based on results of the previous auction. A program ceiling applies to central bank purchases. *Reverse repos:* Introduced in May 1996. Commercial banks can offer to buy treasury bills for up to two weeks at the central bank secondary market rates. There has been little use of this instrument to date.	instrument since February 1994, with the objective of maintaining the exchange rate at its peg to the SDR.

Table 8.3 *(continued)*

	Reserve Requirements	Standing & Nonmarket-Based Discretionary Facilities	Market Operations	Other Instruments
Lithuania	The reserve ratio of 10 percent applies to commercial banks' domestic and foreign currency deposit liabilities, except deposit liabilities with a contractual maturity of less than one year. Effective January 13, 1998, nonresidents will no longer be exempt; the reserve ratio of 5 percent will be raised by 1 percentage point a month so that by July 13, 1998 the reserve ratio will have reached 10 percent. Reserves can be only met by deposits with the central bank; averaging of reserves is allowed for deposits in litas but not for foreign exchange. In case of noncompliance, banks pay a penalty rate of one and a half times the previous month's interbank rate for shortfalls of up to 20 percent of the required reserves; for shortfalls in excess of 20 percent, the fine is two times the overnight rate. Penalty on deficiencies in foreign exchange is 0.2 percent per day. In March 1996, the Bank of Lithuania (BOL) suspended the penalties for reserve shortfalls, and in May 1996 reduced the reserve requirement ratio from 10 percent to 5 percent in	Extension of central bank credit to commercial banks is limited to the amount of foreign exchange reserves in excess of those needed to provide full backing of base money. In this context, the BOL has provided emergency credit to commercial banks on a very limited scale.	*Repurchase operations* in treasury bills were introduced by the BOL in the second quarter of 1997. Multiple-rate auctions *Deposit auctions*: Introduced in the second quarter of 1997 and used on an ad hoc basis.	

	response to the liquidity crisis. The authorities restored the level of bank reserves gradually, raising it by 1 percentage point each quarter, starting in September 1996. The level currently stands at 10 percent. Penalties for reserve shortfalls have been reintroduced since June 1996.		
Moldova	A uniform reserve ratio has been in force since December 1994. In late 1995, the ratio was lowered from 12 percent to 8 percent. The ratio applies to commercial banks' domestic and foreign currency deposits where deposits are averaged over the reserve maintenance period. Required reserves above 5 percent are remunerated at a rate equal to the inflation rate; and banks meet the reserve requirement on average. Foreign currency deposits are also subject to an 8 percent reserve ratio, but this may be satisfied by holding deposits abroad. As of February 1, 1997, domestic currency-denominated vault cash was made eligible as a reserve asset (up to 2 percent of total requirements), and reserves for foreign currency deposits have to be maintained in domestic currency.	*Lombard facility:* Regulations were approved in November 1995; the first Lombard credit was extended in April 1996; short-term central bank credit was originally extended at a highly punitive interest rate that deterred banks' use of this facility. The Lombard rate was lowered in 1997 and established at the level of the 28-day treasury bill discount rate, set at the last auction, plus a 5 percent margin, and the volume of transactions has expanded considerably. Lombard operations have been structured in the form of repurchase agreements of government securities because this structure gives the National Bank of Moldova clearer title to the collateral in the event of a bank default.	*Credit auctions*: In November 1996, all remaining restrictions on the access to credit auctions were eliminated, and access to auctions was limited only for prudential reasons or lack of collateral. Banks can acquire central bank credit up to 25 percent of their liabilities. As of May 1997, the share of auctioned credit to central bank's total credit extended to banks was 90 percent. Interest rates are not sensitive to seasonal factors or the size of the offer, as some of the auctioned credit does not differ substantially from directed credit. Single-price auctions for primary sales of government securities are held on a weekly basis with no minimum rate. Credit auctions are held twice a month; the maturity of auctioned credit will be gradually shortened to 30 days. A transition toward a multiple-price auction in 1998 is under review. *Open market operations:* These operations began in early 1997 and operate on a regular schedule; they are expected to completely replace credit auctions by the end of 1998.

Table 8.3 *(continued)*

	Reserve Requirements	Standing & Nonmarket-Based Discretionary Facilities	Market Operations	Other Instruments
Russia	Reserve requirements are differentiated by type of deposits and currency. On May 1, 1997, they were reduced from 16 percent to 14 percent on ruble deposits of less than 30 days; from 13 percent to 11 percent on ruble deposits of 30 to 90 days; and from 10 percent to 8 percent on ruble deposits of more than 90 days. Furthermore, reserve requirements on foreign currency deposits were increased from 5 percent to 6 percent. For greater uniformity, the savings bank is now subject to a 9.5 percent reserve requirement on household deposits and has established the same reserve requirement for non-household and foreign currency deposits as other banks. In November 1997, the requirement on foreign currency deposits was raised from 6 percent to 9 percent; and in February 1998, it was further raised to 11 percent. Reserve compliance has improved, arising from regulations allowing the Central Bank of Russia to unilaterally transfer balances from correspondent to reserve accounts for delinquent	*Directed credit:* The central bank is no longer providing direct credit through non-market means. *Overdraft:* There are two settlement facilities. The first, through end-of-day repos, provides two-day settlement funds for primary dealers on the securities market. The second, a general settlement over banks' correspondent accounts, is provided on an uncollateralized basis to selected banks. Both are offered at a penalty rate of 1.3 times the refinance rate. *Lombard facility:* The central bank introduced a Lombard facility in 1996. The facility provides 7-, 14-, and 28-day credit, on the basis of predeposited collateral.	*Credit auctions*: Not used since September 1996. *Deposit facility:* Introduced in 1995, and was used on an ad hoc basis, available to Moscow-based primary dealers for overnight, two- and seven-day terms. The deposit facility was recently modified from an auction to a fixed-price offer. *Primary market for treasury bills:* The central bank manages auctions of treasury bills. *Secondary market for treasury bills:* The central bank actively intervenes, buying and selling treasury bills to manage yields. The central bank purchases treasury-bills from the screen-based secondary market at MICEX. *Repo operations:* Repo operations are conducted with primary dealers on treasury bills and federal loan bonds, twice a day.	*Foreign exchange operations:* Purchases are used to provide liquidity to the market on occasion, but are primarily used for exchange rate management.

	banks. Reserve averaging is allowed, but is very restrictive, with a prescribed floor of 95 percent but only from day 5 and 25 of each month. The reserves are unremunerated.			
Tajikistan	As of January 1997, uniform 20 percent ratio applies to all deposits. Penalty for noncompliance is 5 percent of the deficient amount.	The National Bank of Tajikistan operates a standing refinance window. The maturity of refinance credit varies according to type of project and can be as long as two years. The central bank charges the refinance rate, which since December 1997 has been set at the rate of the credit auction plus 0.5 percent per month. Penalty for overdue loans is five times the refinance rate. Directed credits were abolished by presidential decree in July 1997.	*Credit auctions*: Introduced at the end of 1997. The auction format was changed in February 1998 to the multiple-price format.	The central bank's foreign exchange operations have on occasion been used for short-term liquidity management. Limits on cash withdrawals for households were eliminated in February 1987.
Turkmenistan	Since January 1996, the uniform reserve ratio on all deposit liabilities including foreign currency deposits (with the latter exempted in the case of one bank) has been 11 percent; there is a weekly maintenance period. Reserves must be held at the central bank. Since September 1996, 30 percent of vault cash is allowed against reserve requirements. The penalty rate is 0.2 percent of the shortfall daily.	*Central bank credit*: In 1997, the central bank provided refinance credit to commercial banks at the refinance rate. In addition, directed credits were again issued by presidential decree at rates below the Central Bank of Turkmenistan refinance rate to selected industries and agriculture.	*Credit auction:* Auctions that were conducted regularly in 1996 to determine the refinance interest rate were suspended in March 1997 to avoid excessive liquidity expansion. The auction format varies, but the American auction is commonly used.	Foreign exchange auctions are conducted as weekly auctions, but are not used for monetary policy purposes.

Table 8.3 *(concluded)*

	Reserve Requirements	Standing & Nonmarket-Based Discretionary Facilities	Market Operations	Other Instruments
Turkmenistan *(continued)*		*Auxiliary credit facility*: Introduced in 1996 to provide banks with short-term credits at a penalty rate that is linked to the central bank refinance interest rate so that overdrafts can be avoided. These credits are available at a penalty rate of 1.2 times the refinance rate, for a maximum of seven days only. Unauthorized overdrafts are charged 1.7 times the refinance rate.		
Ukraine	From December 1, 1997, a uniform rate of 15 percent has been applied to all domestic and foreign currency deposits. Banks are permitted to use treasury bills to satisfy the increase in reserve requirement from the previous rate of 11 percent. Up to 10 percent of vault cash can be used to cover the reserve requirement. The requirement held in domestic currency is based on contemporaneous reserve accounting, averaged over each 10-day period. The penalty rate of twice the refinance rate in case of shortfalls	*Lombard facility*: Introduced in December 1995. It currently provides fixed-term 10-day advances against treasury bills—the only collateral accepted. The facility provides an interest rate above the refinance rate or the current rate for the securities. There are no quotas, but access is limited to banks with no overdue debt to the National Bank of Ukraine and complying with its regulations.	*Targeted credit auctions:* Phased out in 1996; authorities reported no directed credit operations during 1997. *General credit auctions:* The collateral required for all auctions can be in the form of treasury bills and municipal securities. Held as multiple-price auctions with a minimum interest rate (refinance rate). *Repurchase agreements*: Conducted between the central bank and commercial banks are increasingly used to manage banking system liquidity.	The central bank's foreign exchange operations were conducted on both the auction market and interbank foreign exchange market. There is increasing coordination between monetary/credit operations and foreign exchange operations.

	applies to reserves not meeting the above requirements. Reserves are unremunerated.			
Uzbekistan	The reserve ratio on sum deposits decreased from 30 percent to 25 percent effective June 1996 (10 percent for deposits of more than three years). At the same time, the regulations changed to allow vault cash to count toward fulfilling the requirement. No reserve requirement is imposed on foreign currency deposits. Reserves are unremunerated, and there is no averaging.	*Directed credit:* The Central Bank of Uzbekistan has not extended credit to banks at posted rates since the second quarter of 1995. Directed credit is now being provided through the budget. The central bank stands ready to repurchase its certificates of deposit after they have run for at least two weeks, at a rate to be determined on a case-by-case basis.	*Credit auction*: uses an open outcry method. Banks must comply with prudential regulations and norms to participate in these auctions. Credits are uncollateralized. The scale of operations is growing. *Certificate of deposit auctions:* conducted using sealed bid. The central bank decides what the cutoff rate and volumes will be. The importance of the interbank market is declining as the treasury bill market becomes more active. *Primary market for treasury bills:* Is in place. The central bank conducts open market operations (including repurchase agreements) in the secondary market.	Limits on cash withdrawals have been eliminated. Foreign exchange purchases are used to provide liquidity to the market.

Sources: Country authorities; and IMF.

Table 8.4. Developments in Foreign Exchange, 1997

	Exchange Rate Arrangements and Policy	Market Structure	Regulatory Framework	Central Bank Operations
Armenia	*Arrangement:* Independently floating. *Outcome:* After depreciating by 14 percent during the first five months of 1997, the exchange rate vis-à-vis the U.S. dollar stabilized and appreciated slightly in response to capital inflows and changes in economic conditions. *Gross reserves* increased to 3.1 months of imports by end-1997 compared to 2.2 months at end-1996.	The exchange rate is *unified.* The official rate is set daily by the central bank at the midpoint of previous day's buying and selling rates in the interbank market. The role of *foreign exchange auctions* (daily auctions on the stock exchange) has essentially been eliminated. *Interbank trading* is expanding. Market procedures still need some improvement (reporting of foreign exchange transactions, dealers' association, codes of conduct, and settlement procedures), and developments are under way in these areas. *Foreign exchange bureaus* now have brokerage activities, and the need for bank affiliation was lifted.	*Article VIII status* (May 1997): The *current account* is practically free of restrictions. There is no *surrender requirement* or *repatriation requirement.* There are practically no *capital restrictions,* but authorities retain the power to impose them. *The open position* limit is 40 percent, high in relation to international standards, and is applied only to long positions. Since March 1, 1998, short or long foreign exchange positions have been limited to 40 percent. In addition open positions on currencies other than Swiss francs and those included in ECU and SDR are limited to 10 percent.	*Foreign exchange intervention* is made exclusively through the interbank market, and is *coordinated with monetary policy* (often used as a monetary policy instrument). *Reserve management* is well-advanced. A broad set of investment guidelines has been established with an average maturity up to three months in high-quality institutions; derivatives are prohibited. The Investment Committee reviews decisions fortnightly with daily and weekly reports. *Internal control and administration* of the foreign exchange operations is well organized, and from late 1997 has been combined with domestic operations, with better coordination between back, middle, and front offices.

Azerbaijan	*Arrangement:* Independently floating. *Outcome:* The exchange rate of the manat continued gradually appreciating during 1997. *Gross* reserves increased from 2.0 months of imports in 1996 to 3.8 months in 1997.	The exchange rate is *unified* with the official/cash buying rate spread in the 1–4 percent range during most of 1996. The official exchange rate is set at daily *foreign exchange auctions* in the Baku International Currency Exchange (BICEX) with individuals allowed in 1997 to purchase foreign exchange for bona fide current account transactions. Auctions are transparent, but the settlement of transactions needs to be improved. In August 1997 the Azerbaijan National Bank lifted the prohibition on *interbank market* trading. Cash exchange takes place through licensed *foreign exchange bureaus.* Selling rate should not exceed 5 percent of official rate.	Has not yet achieved *Article VIII status* but under current plans will do so in the context of next Article IV consultation. Progress has been made in eliminating almost all restrictions on current account transactions. There is no *surrender requirement.* The *repatriation requirement* for enterprises that are current in tax payments was abolished in 1996. The restrictions on *capital transactions* seem enforced with a high degree of compliance. *Open position limits* are in place.	*Foreign exchange intervention* occurs through the auction system and the interbank foreign exchange market. It is used to smooth exchange rate movements, and is coordinated with monetary policy (sales are kept broadly consistent with the targeted growth of base money). *Reserve management*: The central bank is responsible for managing foreign exchange and gold reserves. The central bank board has formulated an official reserve management policy. Current practice is to keep virtually all reserves in U.S. dollar deposits in some of the world's largest banks and a few central banks. Some, however, are held in a domestic commercial bank.

Table 8.4 *(continued)*

	Exchange Rate Arrangements and Policy	Market Structure	Regulatory Framework	Central Bank Operations
Belarus	*Arrangement*: Other managed floating. *Outcome*: During 1997 there was a smooth depreciation of exchange rate as a result of interventions on the exchange and use of restrictions on the buying of foreign currency. *Gross reserves* remained below one month of imports in 1996 and 1997.	Foreign currency is allocated predominantly for purchasing strategically important imports (for the most part energy resources). The exchange rate is determined in daily trading sessions on the Interbank Currency Exchange. The Interbank Currency Market legally operates, but in actuality restrictions on formation of exchange rates do not allow it to operate at full volume. On the over-the-counter market, the exchange rate for a transaction may not exceed the unified exchange rate of the National Bank of Belarus and may not be more than 2 percent beneath it. The difference between the official exchange rate and the exchange rate determined on the curb market was as much as 70–80 percent in the first quarter of 1998.	Belarus does not yet have *Article VIII status*. Remaining restrictions give rise to a multiple-currency practice. *Surrender requirement* for export proceeds was reduced to 30 percent in June 1997. There is a *repatriation requirement.* *Capital account flows* are strictly regulated by the central bank. There are *limits on open foreign exchange positions* for banks, but these apply to the difference of short-long open positions separately with regard to freely convertible currency and currencies with limited convertibility.	*Foreign exchange intervention* has been solely through the auction system. *Coordination with monetary policy* needs improvement. *Reserve management* is centralized at the central bank, which continues to deposit part of its foreign exchange reserves in domestic banks. Satisfactory guidelines with respect to currency distribution, acceptable instruments, and limits have been established.

		Since December 1997 operations on the cash foreign currency market have been liberalized.		
Estonia	*Arrangement:* The kroon is pegged to the deutsche mark, which will be replaced by a peg to the euro with the advent of the European Monetary Union. *Outcome*: The currency board arrangement has been successfully maintained, and the exchange rate is stable. *Gross reserves* were at 1.9 months of imports for 1997 compared to 2.5 months in 1996.	The exchange rate was *unified* under the currency board arrangement. Transactions in convertible currencies are freely handled by commercial banks which can quote their own exchange rates.	Estonia accepted *Article VIII status* in August 1994. *There is full convertibility* for all current and virtually all international capital account transactions. *There are no repatriation or surrender requirements.* *Open position limits* are in place: Exposure has been added to risks under capital adequacy regulations. There are no direct limits, except for currencies of non-OECD countries or for currencies of those countries that have not concluded agreements within the IMF's General Arrangements to Borrow (GAB): exposure limited to 5 percent of capital (10 percent for Latvia and Lithuania).	Foreign exchange intervention was *coordinated with monetary policy* according to the currency board arrangement. *Reserve management*: The central bank has a reserve cover in deutsche marks exceeding 130 percent.

Table 8.4 *(continued)*

	Exchange Rate Arrangements and Policy	Market Structure	Regulatory Framework	Central Bank Operations
Georgia	*Arrangement*: Other managed floating. *Outcome*: The lari remained broadly stable against the U.S. dollar during 1997. The National Bank of Georgia was a net purchaser of foreign exchange in the second half of 1997 for the first time since the introduction of the lari in late 1995. *Gross reserves* have fallen to 2.5 months of imports in 1997 from 2.7 months of imports in 1996.	The exchange rate is *unified,* with the official rate set daily on the basis of the auction rate. *Foreign exchange auctions* are well-established, moving to daily frequency in January 1996. The *interbank market* accounts for about 40 percent of total transactions and is growing in part due to increased confidence among banks. Banks with good financial standing conduct half of their transactions in this market, which is cheaper than the Tbilisi Interbank Currency Exchange (TICEX), where an official fee is applied. A code of conduct is under preparation. *Foreign exchange bureaus* can buy and sell cash since 1993.	Georgia accepted *Article VIII status* in December 1996. The exchange system is free of restrictions on current and capital accounts, although *capital flows* are subject to a registration requirement for monitoring. *There are no surrender or repatriation requirements.* *Open position limits* are now strictly enforced and are backed by penalties of 0.1 percent per day. Limits were reduced to 20 percent for aggregate positions (from 25 percent) and to zero for individual positions (from 10 percent), effective December 1997.	*Foreign exchange intervention* through auctions in TICEX, and has been one of the main instruments of monetary policy and of exchange rate management, consistent with meeting reserve targets under the IMF program. *Reserve management*: The central bank is well advanced in managing reserves, and has established a reserve management committee. Investment is mainly in secure short-term deposits, with some diversification in treasury bills already started. *Internal control and administration*: The central bank has set up a dealing room separated from the back office.
Kazakhstan	*Arrangement*: Managed floating. *Outcome*: The tenge has been stable in nominal terms during most of 1997.	The exchange rate is *unified.* Official exchange rate set weekly by the Technical Committee for Monetary and Exchange Policy based on the daily auction rate	Kazakhstan accepted *Article VIII status* in July 1996. *There is no surrender requirement. Repatriation requirements* remain unless a	*Foreign exchange intervention* has been mainly in the auction market. The central bank also intervenes in the interbank market, but

Gross reserves rose slightly to 3.2 months of imports in 1997 from 3.1 months in 1996.	and interbank market rates, which differ only slightly from the rate of the foreign exchange bureaus. *Interbank trading* is developing well with market share representing 65 percent of total foreign exchange transactions during the period from January to September 1997, compared to 56 percent in 1996. A code of conduct for dealers was adopted in 1997, and the establishment of a dealers' association is under discussion. *The foreign exchange bureau market* is fairly significant with 2,135 licenced foreign exchange bureaus.	special license is issued by the National Bank of Kazakhstan with the approval of the ministry of finance (if the amount exceeds the equivalent of US$100,000) and the Strategic Planning and Reform Agency (if the amount exceeds the equivalent of US$10 million). *Capital account transactions* involving an outflow of capital from the republic (direct and portfolio investments abroad, and credits and loans to nonresidents for a period of more than 180 days) and carried out in foreign currency shall be licensed by the central bank. Capital inflows (direct and portfolio investments in Kazakhstan, and credits and loans received by residents for a period of more than 180 days) in excess of the equivalent of US$100,000 shall be subject to registration with the central bank. *Open position limits* of 30 percent of capital for individual currencies; and 50 percent for aggregate positions with daily reporting to the central bank required. Limits were not consistently observed.	less frequently, depending on exchange rate and timing. *Reserve management*: An investment committee was established and limits to risk exposure were adopted in 1997. *Internal control and administration* were strengthened by establishing a clear distinction between the back and front offices.

Table 8.4 *(continued)*

	Exchange Rate Arrangements and Policy	Market Structure	Regulatory Framework	Central Bank Operations
Kyrgyz Republic	*Arrangement:* Other managed floating. *Outcome*: Since May 1997 the som has remained broadly stable. Overall, it depreciated by 4.18 percent between January and October 1997. *Gross reserves* increased from 1.7 months of imports at the end of 1996 to 3.3 months at end-1997.	The exchange rate is *unified.* The official exchange rate is determined in twice-weekly *foreign exchange auctions* at the central bank. The method for holding the auctions was changed to a multiple-price mechanism in February 1998. The official rate of the central bank is the weighted average of the auction price. Turnover at the auction fell further in 1997 ($37 million from January to September 1997 compared to $97 million in 1996). *Limited interbank trading* (amounted to 39 percent of the total foreign exchange transactions from January to August 1997).	Kyrgyz Republic accepted *Article VIII status* in March 1995 with full *capital and current account convertibility.* *There are no surrender* or *repatriation* requirements. *Open position limits* are in place (15 percent and 30 percent on individual and aggregate currency positions respectively).	*Foreign exchange intervention* is through auctions, mainly the sale of donor funds, primarily for the purpose of limiting exchange rate fluctuations, and to adjust banking system liquidity. *Reserves management:* Investment Committee was established in 1994, guidelines for portfolio composition and permissible investments strengthened in 1997. *Internal control and administration*: Good progress has been made with clear separation of back and front offices. More back-office training is needed.

Latvia	*Arrangement*: The lats is pegged to the SDR. *Outcome*: The lats has adjusted slightly against the U.S. dollar. The authorities remained committed to the peg as a cornerstone of monetary policy. *Gross reserves* fell slightly to 3.0 months of imports in 1997.	The exchange rate is *unified.* The Bank of Latvia reviews domestic and international exchange markets on a daily basis, and announces daily buying and selling rates for the lats. *Interbank trading* is developing, with trading among commercial banks taking place through a telephone system. An informal dealers' committee was set up in 1995.	Latvia accepted *Article VIII status* in June 1994. Current and capital account transactions have been fully liberalized. There are no surrender or *repatriation requirements.* *Open position limits* are 10 percent for each currency and 20 percent on aggregate.	*Foreign exchange intervention* is conducted in the interbank market. *Reserves management* is relatively well advanced with an investment committee meeting weekly. There has been a gradual move to active management of reserves. *Internal control and administration* has been strengthened with clearer distinction between front and back offices, and stronger market monitoring.
Lithuania	*Arrangement*: The litas is pegged to the U.S. dollar under a currency board arrangement. In view of the integration into the EU, exit strategy from the currency board arrangement is envisaged. The Bank of Lithuania has adopted a three-stage monetary policy program from 1997 to 1999 in support of reorientation of the peg to the euro. *Outcome*: The litas has been stable against the dollar. *Gross reserves* increased to 2.9 months of imports.	The exchange rate was *unified* under the currency board arrangement. Banks authorized to trade in foreign exchange are allowed to transact among themselves, as well as with residents and nonresidents.	Lithuania accepted *Article VIII status* in May 1994. *There is full convertibility* for all current and capital account transactions. There are no *repatriation* or *surrender requirements.* *Open position limits* on banks were 30 percent on aggregate positions and 20 percent for individual currencies.	*Foreign exchange intervention* has been in accordance with the currency board arrangement, which also governs *coordination with monetary policy.*

Table 8.4 *(continued)*

	Exchange Rate Arrangements and Policy	Market Structure	Regulatory Framework	Central Bank Operations
Moldova	*Arrangement*: Independently floating. *Outcome*: The exchange rate of the leu has been relatively stable against the U.S. dollar with a slight depreciation in the latter part of 1997. *Gross reserves* increased to 3.9 months of imports with limited amounts of net intervention by the National Bank of Moldova.	The exchange rate is *unified.* The official exchange rate is determined in daily fixing sessions of the Chisinau Interbank Foreign Currency Exchange (CIFCE) *auctions*. The spread between cash and noncash rates is insignificant. The *interbank market* has developed steadily and soundly (98 percent of total turnover). A revised code of conduct has been adopted by a majority of commercial banks. There is no dealers' association. *Foreign exchange bureaus* in the cash market are active and functioning well.	Moldova accepted *Article VIII* status in June 1995. The leu is *freely convertible in current account* transactions. *There are no surrender requirements. Repatriation requirements* remain. *Capital accounts* remain restricted with rather strict licensing requirements from the central bank; capital inflows are treated liberally. *Open position limits* on banks were 25 percent on aggregate positions.	*Foreign exchange intervention* is conducted through auctions and partly in interbank market. The Monetary and Foreign Exchange Committee meets at least weekly to determine the mix of monetary and foreign exchange operations. *Reserve management*: The central bank has full responsibility for managing foreign exchange reserves. Investments are made properly with prudential rules fully respected. *Internal control and administration*: The foreign exchange operations section is properly structured with separate front, middle, and back offices. There are suitable equipment and a skilled staff. Reporting procedures are in place.

Russia	*Arrangement*: Other managed floating. On July 1, 1996 the Central Bank of Russia switched to a sliding band regime. Announced band for 1997 slid from Rub 5,500–6,100 in January to Rub 5,750–6,350 at year-end. To stabilize the exchange rate on a short-term basis, the central bank announces daily a narrower intervention band. For the period 1998–2000 the central bank has announced a central rate of new Rub 6.2 per U.S. dollar, with a margin of ±15 percent (compared to about ±5 percent under the 1997 regime). *Outcome*: The central bank has maintained an increase in inflows of foreign capital. An outflow of foreign capital at the beginning of the year was of a temporary nature. *Gross reserves* increased from two months of imports in 1996 to 2.4 months in 1997.	The exchange rate is *unified*. The official exchange rate is determined by the central bank in relation to bid-ask quotations of more than 20 large banks in the interbank market. *Interbank trading* is active. A government tax was imposed on net turnover at Moscow Interbank Foreign Currency Exchange (MICEX), which led to a further shift toward the interbank market. Market share was about 80 percent of total transactions at end-1996. Interbank trading in foreign exchange derivatives occurs only in Moscow.	Russia accepted *Article VIII status* in June 1996. Liberalization of foreign access to treasury bill market will be completed in 1998 with the lifting of all remaining restrictions of nonresident investment in the government securities market. *Surrender requirement*: 50 percent of export proceeds must be sold through authorized banks. There is a *repatriation requirement* of 100 percent. Enforcement of *capital restrictions* is monitored by the central bank. *Open exposure limits* are not consistent with international practice. Some progress has occurred in making such limits more effective.	*Foreign exchange intervention* is conducted both in MICEX and the interbank market to smooth out fluctuations in the exchange rate within the band. Greater *coordination with monetary policy* is needed. *Reserve management*: The central bank is responsible for managing official reserves, while a small part of the official reserves are managed by the Ministry of Finance and part are deposited in former Soviet sectoral banks abroad; authorities wish to centralize reserves at the central bank, although no new development reported. Reserves held at the central bank are managed with clear separation of functions.

Table 8.4 *(continued)*

	Exchange Rate Arrangements and Policy	Market Structure	Regulatory Framework	Central Bank Operations
Tajikistan	*Arrangement*: Independently floating. The official rate has been kept fixed since May 1997. *Outcome*: The exchange rate depreciated sharply during 1997 (from TR 330 per U.S. dollar at end-1996 to an estimated TR 800 by end-1997). *Gross reserves* remained below one month of imports in 1997.	The exchange rate is *unified*; however, from end-1996, foreign exchange has been increasingly allocated through directed credit. The National Bank of Tajikistan stopped auctions; the Tajikistan Interbank Foreign Currency Exchange (the TICEX) virtually ceased to function; and the official rate became set administratively. The commercial bank rate spread over the official rate was stable at around 25 percent on average during 1997. Weekly auctions were restarted in July and since then NBT has unified the cash and noncash auctions. However, lack of transparency in auctions resulted in continuing segmentation between the curb market and auctions. *Interbank trading* is permitted but it attracts limited interest.	Tajikistan has not yet accepted *Article VIII status*. Import and export duties were reinstated during the first half of 1997. There is *no surrender requirement*, but there is a *repatriation requirement*. There are some *capital account restrictions*. *Open position limits* were to be introduced in 1998.	*Foreign exchange interventions* have been conducted through weekly auctions, and are currently aimed at supporting the exchange rate. *Reserve management*: The central bank has full control of foreign exchange reserves. Guidelines need to be further enhanced. *Internal control and administration*: There is no back office with proper facilities for confirmation. Also, there is no clear separation of responsibilities. There is a clear need for improvement in skills, better correspondent account management, and internal reporting.

Turkmenistan	*Arrangement*: Other managed floating. *Outcome*: The official rate has been fixed since May 1997; however, a growing spread emerged with bank cash rate, which approximates the curb market rate. *Gross reserves* rose significantly to 16 months of imports in 1997 from about 9 months in 1996.	The official exchange rate was *unified* at the bank market rate on January 1, 1996, but a *dual system* was reintroduced in February until April. The official rate was established at the *weekly foreign exchange auctions*; however, access is restricted and certain transactions are excluded. The *commercial bank* rate spread over the official rate was stable at around 30 percent during 1997. On April 13, 1998 the central bank announced the introduction of a unified exchange rate. *Interbank trading* has been allowed since end-1995, but has been subject to restrictions on the size of the transactions; the volume of trading remains extremely thin.	Turkmenistan has not yet accepted *Article VIII status*. A number of exchange restrictions have been maintained, some of them giving rise to multiple-currency practice. Bilateral and trilateral payment arrangements remain. *Surrender requirements* have been unified at 50 percent and have been eliminated for joint venture and private sector firms in 1997. Also elimination of surrender requirement of oil/gas exports to the Foreign Exchange Reserve Fund. *Capital account restrictions* are enforced. *Open position limits* will be introduced in 1998.	*Reserve management*: The Central Bank of Turkmenistan does not have full control over official reserves, but retains responsibility for oversight of their management, which is largely entrusted to several major western banks. *Internal control and administration*: Back and front offices are separated. Improvements in payments and communications systems were introduced in 1997, and a major upgrade is under way that will involve the establishment of an electronic settlement system.

Table 8.4 *(concluded)*

	Exchange Rate Arrangements and Policy	Market Structure	Regulatory Framework	Central Bank Operations
Ukraine	*Arrangement*: Other managed floating. The band for the exchange rate widened from HRV 1.7–1.9 per U.S. dollar at the end of 1997 to HRV 1.8–2.25 in 1998. *Outcome*: The exchange rate was stable against the U.S. dollar during most of 1997. However, a change in market sentiment at the end of 1997 resulted in pressures on the exchange rate with capital outflows from the treasury bill market. *Gross reserves* increased from 1.1 weeks of imports at end-1996 to 1.4 weeks by end-1997.	The exchange rate is *unified.* The official exchange rate is determined through competitive bidding of commercial banks at daily auctions of the National Bank of Ukraine. *Interbank trading* is allowed to take place within a margin of ±0.3 percent around the official rate. Turnover in the interbank market is larger than the auction market. The *foreign exchange bureau* was introduced in 1995. A maximum spread of 10 percent was imposed between the official rate and the cash rate quoted by the bureaus.	Ukraine accepted *Article VIII status* in September 1996. *Surrender requirements* were abolished in 1997. *Repatriation requirements* remain. Authorities intend to gradually remove restrictions on *capital transactions.* In 1997 restrictions were lifted for residents to borrow foreign exchange from nonresidents. *Open position limits* are in place. New regulations are under preparation that will limit overall exposure to 40 percent of bank capital and 20 percent for individual currencies.	*Foreign exchange intervention* has been conducted on the interbank market only since end-1996, and is aimed at smoothing short-term exchange rate fluctuations. *Reserve management*: The central bank has widened the spectrum of operations in order to enhance effectiveness of management. The main instruments are short- and long-term deposits, government securities, and investments entrusted to external managers. *Internal control and administration:* Over the past year the central bank has been developing its own system of assets management that meets international standards and provides for risk assessment.

Uzbekistan	*Arrangement*: Other managed floating. *Outcome*: The exchange system came under pressure by mid-1996 in light of a deteriorating economic situation and the Central Bank of Uzbekistan let the official rate depreciate to some extent. Depreciation continued in 1997 though at a slower pace. *Gross reserves* decreased from 5.4 months of imports at end-1996 to about 3.6 months by end-1997.	Exchange rate is not unified: (i) certain importers and transactions (e.g., industrial exporters) have access to centralized foreign exchange resources through central bank *auctions;* (ii) importers of some consumer goods can obtain foreign exchange at the more depreciated *commercial bank rate* and for other consumer goods only through the illegal *curb market;* (iii) buying-selling rates for cash transactions of *foreign exchange bureaus* are administratively set below the official rate (12 percent discount). These practices give rise to multiple-currency practice. The official exchange rate is determined weekly based on the central bank auction rates. The frequency of auctions was raised from weekly to daily in March 1997.	Uzbekistan has not yet accepted *Article VIII status.* After an initial liberalization in late 1995, the exchange system was severely restricted in late-1996, creating a segmented foreign exchange market. Foreign currency receipts from exports of goods and services are subject to a 30 percent surrender requirement. Receipts in convertible currency from centralized exports of gold and cotton are subject to 100 percent surrender to the central bank at the official exchange rate. There are some restrictions on *capital account transactions.* *Open position limits* are in place (20 percent of statutory capital).	*Foreign exchange intervention* is conducted through the auction system. *Reserve management* is effected by the central bank, although in a number of instances the National Bank for Foreign Economic Activity may act as an agent. Reserves are kept in precious metals and freely convertible currency.

Sources: Country authorities; and IMF.

Table 8.5. Priorities for Future Reform in the Foreign Exchange Area

	Armeria	Azerbaijan	Belarus	Estonia	Georgia	Kazakhstan	Kyrgyz Republic	Lativa	Lithuania	Moldova	Russia	Tajikistan	Turkmenistan	Ukraine	Uzbekistan
Interbank foreign exchange market															
Permission of outside auction transactions			•												•
Modification of surrender requirement			•								•	•	•		•
Open position limits[1]			•		•	•					•		•		
Adoption of code of conduct and market rules	•	•	•				•					•	•		•
Foreign exchange reserve management															
Basic investment strategy and policy		•		•								•	•		•
Centralization of management at central bank or terminating placement with domestic banks			•								•		•		•
Exchange and monetary operations coordination															
Harmonization of a decision making process			•								•	•	•		•
Current account convertibility															
Elimination of other restrictions including bilateral payments arrangements and multiple currency practices		•	•									•	•		•
Acceptance of Article VIII obligations		•	•									•	•		•
Capital account convertibility[2]		•				•				•				•	

Source: IMF.

[1]Bullet marks on this criterion indicate that open position limits are not imposed, or are not strictly enforced, or are large compared with international standards (which tend to be about 15 percent and 30 percent on individual currency and aggregate positions, respectively).

[2]Bullet marks on this criterion imply that the design of a strategy for an orderly liberalization of capital account transactions should be a priority measure.

Table 8.6. Legal and Regulatory Framework for Banking Supervision

	Armenia		Azerbaijan		Belarus		Estonia		Georgia	
	1996	1997	1996	1997	1996	1997	1996	1997	1996	1997
Central bank as the supervisory authority	yes	yes	yes	yes	yes	yes	yes	yes	yes	yes
Number of supervisory staff	55	53	14	39	55	52	22	20	24	25
Banking supervision staff/number of banks (in percent)	167	177	10	38	145	149	157	167	39	47
Authority of supervisory agency to exercise:										
Binding corrective order	yes	yes	yes	yes	yes	yes	yes	yes	yes	yes
Removal of managers	no	yes	yes	yes	yes	yes	yes	yes	yes	yes
Conservatorship	yes	yes	yes	yes	yes	yes	yes	yes	yes	yes
Withdrawal of license	yes	yes	yes	yes	yes	yes	yes	yes	yes	yes
Liquidation	yes	yes	yes	yes	yes	yes	yes	yes	yes	yes
Forced merger	no	no	no	no	. . .	. . .	yes	yes	no	yes
Prudential regulations										
Capital adequacy ratio (in percent)	. . .	5	. . .	10	. . .	10	. . .	10	. . .	10[1]
Risk-weighted capital/asset ratio	yes	yes	yes	yes	yes	yes	yes	yes	no	no
Liquidity ratios	yes	yes	yes	yes	yes	yes	yes	yes	yes	yes
Maximum exposure to single borrower (percent of capital)	. . .	25	. . .	25	. . .	20	. . .	25	. . .	15
Related party lending limits (percent of capital)	. . .	10	. . .	10	. . .	20	. . .	10	. . .	50[2]
Consolidated supervision	yes[3]	yes[3]	no	yes	no	yes	yes	yes	yes	yes
Open foreign exchange position limits	yes	yes	yes	yes	yes	yes	yes	yes	yes	yes
Limits on equity holdings in nonfinancial enterprises (percent of capital)	yes	yes	yes	10	yes	10	yes	15[4]	yes	20
Loan classification and provisioning	yes	yes	yes	yes	yes	yes	yes	yes	yes	yes
Internal control or audit	yes	yes	yes	yes	yes	yes	yes	yes	yes	yes
Suspension of interest accrual on overdue loans	yes	yes	yes	yes	yes	yes	yes	yes	yes	yes

Table 8.6 *(continued)*

	Armenia		Azerbaijan		Belarus		Estonia		Georgia	
	1996	1997	1996	1997	1996	1997	1996	1997	1996	1997
Accounting and legal framework										
Broadly adapted financial statements	yes	yes	yes	yes	yes	yes	yes	yes	no	yes
Adopted International Accounting Standards	no	yes	no	yes	yes	yes	yes	yes	no	no
Commercial banking law	yes	yes	yes	yes	yes	yes	yes	yes	yes	yes
Central bank law	yes	yes	yes	yes	yes	yes	yes	yes	yes	yes
Civil code										
Property rights	yes	yes	yes	yes	yes	yes	yes	yes	yes	yes
Law on contracts	yes	yes	yes	yes	yes	yes	. . .	under preparation	yes	yes
Law on collateral	yes[5]	yes[5]	yes	yes	yes	yes	. . .	. . .	yes	yes
Law on loan collection	yes[6]	yes[6]	yes	yes	yes	yes	. . .	yes	yes	yes
Bankruptcy law	yes[5]	yes[5]	yes	yes	yes	yes	yes	yes	yes	yes
Separate provisions for banks	yes	yes	no	yes	yes	yes	yes	yes	yes	yes
Money laundering law	yes[7]	yes[7]	no	no	no	no	under preparation	under preparation	. . .	no

Table 8.6 *(continued)*

	Kazakhstan		Kyrgyz Republic		Latvia		Lithuania		Moldova	
	1996	1997	1996	1997	1996	1997	1996	1997	1996	1997
Central bank as the supervisory authority	yes	yes	yes	yes	yes	yes	yes	yes	yes	yes
Number of supervisory staff	117	109	42	44	55	55	53	54	45	48
Banking supervision staff/number of banks (in percent)	116	111	233	244	167	172	133	104	214	218
Authority of supervisory agency to exercise										
Binding corrective order	yes	yes	yes	yes	yes	yes	yes	yes	yes	yes
Removal of managers	no	no	yes	yes	yes	yes	yes	yes	yes	yes
Conservatorship	yes	yes	yes	yes	yes	yes	yes	yes	yes	yes
Withdrawal of license	yes	yes	yes	yes	yes	yes	yes	yes	yes	yes
Liquidation	yes	no	yes	yes	yes	yes	yes	yes	yes	yes
Forced merger	no	no	no	no	no	no	yes	yes	yes	yes
Prudential regulations										
Capital adequacy ratio (in percent)	. . .	8	. . .	8	yes	10	13	10	. . .	8
Risk weighted capital/asset ratio	yes	yes	yes	yes	yes	yes	yes	yes	yes	yes
Liquidity ratios	yes	yes	yes	yes	yes	yes	yes	yes	yes	yes
Maximum exposure to single borrower (percent of capital)	. . .	25	25	25	. . .	25	30	25	. . .	30
Related party lending limits (percent of capital)	. . .	10	15	15	. . .	15	10	10	. . .	20
Consolidated supervision	no	yes[8]	yes	yes	yes	yes	yes	yes	yes	yes
Open foreign exchange position limits	yes	yes	yes	yes	yes	yes	yes	yes	yes	yes
Limits on equity holdings in nonfinancial enterprises (percent of capital)	yes[9]	10	yes	15	yes	15[4]	yes	10	no	yes
Loan classification and provisioning	yes	yes	yes	yes	yes	yes	yes	yes	yes	yes
Internal control/audit	yes	yes	yes	yes	yes	yes	yes	yes	. . .	yes
Suspension of interest accrual on overdue loans	yes	yes	yes	yes	yes	yes	yes	yes	. . .	yes

Table 8.6 ***(continued)***

	Kazakhstan		Kyrgyz Republic		Latvia		Lithuania		Moldova	
	1996	1997	1996	1997	1996	1997	1996	1997	1996	1997
Accounting and legal framework										
Broadly adapted financial statements	yes	yes	yes	yes	yes	yes	yes	yes	yes	yes
International Accounting Standards	yes	yes	yes	yes	yes	yes	yes	yes	no	yes[10]
Commercial banking law	yes	yes	yes	yes	yes	yes	yes	yes	yes	yes
Central bank law	yes	yes	yes	yes	yes	yes	yes	yes	yes	yes
Civil code										
Property rights	yes	yes	yes	yes	yes	yes	. . .	. . .	yes	yes
Law on contracts	yes	yes	yes	yes	yes	yes	. . .	. . .	yes	yes
Law on collateral	yes[11]	yes	yes	yes	no	yes	no	no	yes	yes
Law on loan collection	yes[12]	yes	yes[13]	yes[13]	yes	yes	. . .	. . .	yes	yes
Bankruptcy law	yes	yes	yes	yes	yes	yes	yes	yes	yes	yes
Separate provisions for banks	no	yes	yes	yes	yes	yes	yes	yes	yes	yes
Money laundering law	no	no	. . .	yes[14]	. . .	yes	prepared	yes[15]	. . .	. . .

Table 8.6 *(continued)*

	Russia		Tajikistan		Turkmenistan		Ukraine		Uzbekistan	
	1996	1997	1996	1997	1996	1997	1996	1997	1996	1997
Central bank as the supervisory authority	yes	yes	yes	yes	yes	yes	yes	yes	yes	yes
Number of supervisory staff	4,100[16]	4,500[16]	14	23	35	45	60[17]	130	68	68
Banking supervision staff/number of banks (in percent)	202	269	61	88	233	67	26	58	234	234
Authority of supervisory agency to exercise:										
Binding corrective order	yes	yes	yes	yes	yes	yes	yes[18]	yes[18]	yes	yes
Removal of managers	yes	partial[19]	yes	yes	yes	yes	yes[18]	yes[18]	yes	yes
Conservatorship	yes	yes	yes	yes	yes	yes	yes[18]	yes[18]	yes	yes
Withdrawal of license	yes	yes	yes	yes	yes	yes	yes[18]	yes[18]	yes	yes
Liquidation	no[20]	yes	yes	yes	yes	yes	yes[18]	yes[18]	yes	yes
Forced merger	no	no	yes	yes	yes	yes	no	no	no	no
Prudential regulations										
Capital adequacy ratio (in percent)	. . .	7	. . .	8	. . .	8	. . .	5	8	8
Risk weighted capital/asset ratio	yes	yes	yes	yes	yes	yes	yes	yes	yes	yes
Liquidity ratios	yes	yes	yes	yes	yes	yes	yes	yes	yes	yes
Maximum exposure to single borrower (percent of capital)	. . .	25	. . .	25	. . .	20	. . .	25	. . .	25
Related party lending limits (percent of capital)	. . .	25	. . .	15	. . .	yes	. . .	25	. . .	15
Consolidated supervision	no[21]	yes[22]	yes[8]	yes	yes	yes	yes	yes	yes	yes
Open foreign exchange position limits	yes	yes	yes	yes	no	yes[23]	yes	yes	yes	yes
Limits on equity holdings in nonfinancial enterprises (percent of capital)	yes	no[24]	no	. . .	no	10[23]	yes	25	yes	15
Loan classification and provisioning	yes	yes	no	no	yes	yes	yes	yes	yes	yes
Internal control/audit	yes	yes	yes	yes	yes	yes	yes	yes	yes	yes
Suspension of interest accrual on overdue loans	no	yes[22]	no	no	yes	yes	no	yes[25]	. . .	yes

Table 8.6 *(concluded)*

	Russia		Tajikistan		Turkmenistan		Ukraine		Uzbekistan	
	1996	1997	1996	1997	1996	1997	1996	1997	1996	1997
Accounting and legal framework										
Broadly adapted financial statements	yes	yes	no	no	yes	yes[23]	no	no	. . .	yes
International Accounting Standards	no	partial	no	no	no	yes[23]	no	no	no	yes
Commercial banking law	yes	yes	yes	yes	yes	yes	yes	yes	yes	yes
Central bank law	yes	yes	yes	yes	yes	yes	. . .[26]	yes[26]	yes	yes
Civil code										
Property rights	yes	yes	yes	yes	yes	yes	. . .	yes	. . .	yes
Law on contracts	yes	yes	yes	yes	no	yes	. . .	yes	. . .	yes
Law on collateral	yes	yes	yes	yes	yes	yes	. . .	yes	yes	yes
Law on loan collection	no	no	yes	yes	no	no	. . .	yes	. . .	no
Bankruptcy law	yes	yes	yes[27]	yes[27]	yes[28]	yes	yes	yes	yes	yes
Separate provisions for banks	no	no	yes[27]	yes[27]	yes	yes	no	no	yes	yes
Money laundering law	no	under preparation	yes[27]	under preparation	no	no	. . .	yes[29]	. . .	no

Sources: Central banks; and IMF.

[1]Total capital to total assets. 8 percent is for Tier 1 capital to total assets.

[2]National Bank of Georgia plans to decrease the limit to 25 percent.

[3]Including branches and subsidiary financial enterprises (excluding Moscow branch of Anelik Bank).

[4]15 percent for each customer, 60 percent of total equity holdings.

[5]Armenia has a separate law.

[6]There are laws on debt collection but not specifically on loan collection.

[7]Incorporated in Banks and Banking Act.

[8]Including branches and subsidiary financial enterprises.

[9]Only investment banks are authorized to have holdings in nonfinancial enterprises.

[10]Introduced in the National Bank of Moldova on July 1, 1995. Since January 1998 commercial banks will transfer to the new chart of accounts based on IAS.

[11]The specific law is no longer in force, but the relevant provisions are included in the civil code.

[12] There is no specific law, but legislation in force does stipulate procedures and means of compulsory debt collection.

[13]Included in central bank regulations and law on collateral.
[14]Specific law on money laundering is being developed, and provisions exist within the commercial banking law.
[15] Law on prevention of money laundering adopted on June 19, 1997.
[16] Includes staff of central bank office and 89 regional branches.
[17] Only central bank office; branches also perform supervisory functions.
[18] National Bank of Ukraine does not exercise the authority (unless license is withdrawn).
[19] The Central Bank of Russia is entitled to place dismissal requirements on the owners of a bank.
[20]The Central Bank of Russia can take the case to court to initiate liquidation.
[21]Supervision includes branches.
[22]To be introduced in 1998.
[23]Scheduled for 1998.
[24]Limits are in effect on a stake in the capital of any organization. Proposed to establish limits individually on a stake in the capital of nonfinancial institutions.
[25]Accrued in a separate off-balance sheet account.
[26]Not a special central bank law but a regulation under the Law on Banks and Banking Activities.
[27]Related provisions are included in the new Central Bank Law.
[28]Not functioning.
[29]Ratification of Strasbourg Convention.

Table 8.7. Structure and Performance of the Banking Sector

	Armenia[1]			Azerbaijan			Belarus			Estonia		
	1995	1996	1997	1995	1996	1997	1995	1996	1997	1995	1996	10/97
Number of banks, of which:	35	33	30	180	136	102	40	38	38	18	14	12
Majority state-owned	1	. . .	1	4	4	4	6	6	4	2	0	0
Foreign	3	4 (including 1 branch)	5	1	3	3	2	2	1	4	4	1
Total assets (in percent of GDP)	8	11	13	37[2]	32	24	13	13	30	36	43	59
Share of five largest banks in total assets (in percent)	65	68	71	>81	>83	75	. . .	62	83	75	78	87
Total loans (in percent of GDP)	4	5	6	18	10	10	6	8	18	15	22	. . .
Total deposits (in percent of GDP)	6	7	8	7	5	20	7	11	13	21	27	. . .
Central bank credit to banks (in percent of GDP)	1	<1	<1	3	2	2.5	4	4	5	1	<1	<1
Average capital adequacy ratio	17	15	14	. . .	3	. . .	. . .	16	12	16	12	12
Nonperforming loans (in percent of total loans)	33	27	12	13[2]	34	29	10	11	10	2	2	1
Share of five largest banks in nonperforming loans (in percent)	90	85	82	. . .	90	90	. . .	76	86	64	80	87

	Georgia			Kazakhstan			Kyrgyz Republic			Latvia		
	1995	1996	11/97	1995	1996	1997	1995	1996	10/97	1995	1996	6/97
Number of banks, of which:	101	61	53	130	101	82	18	18	18	40	33	32
Majority state-owned	. . .	. . .	0	5	5	6	2	4	4	2	2	2
Foreign	. . .	12	14	6	7	20[3]	6	3	3	1	3	5
Total assets (in percent of GDP)	11.9	5	6.7	21.9	11.9	9.5	16	6	10	31	38	45
Share of five largest banks in total assets (in percent)	70	50	43	>80	>59	62	73	72	62	43	44	54
Total loans (in percent of GDP)	4	3	4	6	4	4	10	3	4	8	7	12
Total deposits (in percent of GDP)	2	2	3	6	5	5	5	4	6	12	12	28
Central bank credit to banks (in percent of GDP)	. . .	<1	<1	1	<1	<1	7	<1	<1	<1	1	1
Average capital adequacy ratio	4	8	10	3	13	18	4	8	8[4]	22	25	30
Nonperforming loans (in percent of total loans)	31	10	8	15	20	7	63	22	1	19	18	10
Share of five largest banks in nonperforming loans (in percent)	91	52	17	21	29	39	95	68	30	65	64	57

Table 8.7 *(concluded)*

	Lithuania			Moldova			Russia			Tajikistan		
	1995	1996	1997	1995	1996	10/97	1995	1996	10/97	1995	1996	1997
Number of banks, of which:	16	12	11	20	21	22	2,295	2,030	1,717	19	23	26
Majority state-owned	3	3	3	0	0	0	3	3	3[5]	1	1	2
Foreign	. . .	. . .	1	2	1	1	11	13	14	2	2[6]	2
Total assets (in percent of GDP)	20	25	38	28	33	34	30	28	38	88	14	14
Share of five largest banks in total assets (in percent)	76	79	84	78	70	73	32	39	37	41	90	90
Total loans (in percent of GDP)	14	15	21	13	15	15	13	11	11	15	4	7
Total deposits (in percent of GDP)	14	17	28	8	8	9	16	16	13	16	4	8
Central bank credit to banks (in percent of GDP)	4	1	<1	5	4	2	1	<1	<1	3	2	23
Average capital adequacy ratio (actual)	. . .	11	11	4	4	6	4	5	7[7]	2	8	8
Nonperforming loans (in percent of total loans)	. . .	32	28	9	8	11	7	7	5	4	8	8
Share of five largest banks in nonperforming loans (in percent)	56	71	87	74	68	77	32	31	57	. . .	74	74

	Turkmenistan[8]		Ukraine			Uzbekistan		
	1996	9/97	1995	1996	1997	1995	1996	10/97
Number of banks, of which:	15	67[9]	230	228 (188 active)	225 (189 active)	18	29	29
Majority state-owned	2	2	. . .	. . .	2	10	1	5
Foreign	4	3	. . .	14[10]	19[11]	. . .	. . .	4
Total assets (in percent of GDP)	73	74	37	46	66	19	64	80
Share of five largest banks in total assets (in percent)	72	98	. . .	. . .	57	. . .	93	64
Total loans (in percent of GDP)	40	63	10	5–8	21	19	22	61
Total deposits (in percent of GDP)	5	<1	2	5–8	10	. . .	24	4
Central bank credit to banks (in percent of GDP)	13	7	1	<1	1.4	. . .	4	6
Average capital adequacy ratio (actual)	32	128	4	19	19	. . .	<1	<1
Nonperforming loans (in percent of total loans)	6	3	13	12	11	8[2]	2	4
Share of five largest banks in nonperforming loans (in percent)	92	99	85	77	66	90	56	87

Sources: Central banks of the Baltic countries, Russia, and other countries of the former Soviet Union.

[1]The average capital adequacy ratios for Armenia, which simply total recorded capital divided by total recorded assets, are misleading. In particular, the 1995 and 1996 numbers do not take account of large amounts of nonperforming loans against which provisions, and/or write-offs, were scheduled to be phased in over the two years to end-1997. A better indication is total capital-to-risk-weighted assets, both adjusted for the volume of weighted classified loans. This ratio was –9.7 percent at mid-1996, +12.3 percent at the end of 1996, and + 25.5 percent at end-1997.

[2]Data as of 1994.

[3]The grouping of second-tier banks was changed, by amending the law "On Bank and Banking Activity in the Republic of Kazakhstan" on July 11, 1997.

[4]In the Kyrgyz Republic, total capital/risk-weighted assets times 100 percent.

[5]Included are banks in which over 50 percent of the shares in authorized capital are held by the Central Bank of Russia and the Russian Federation's Federal Property Fund.

[6]Branches of foreign banks.

[7]Minimum requirements as of January 1, 1998, not actual.

[8]No data available for 1995.

[9]Includes branches of Agricultural Bank.

[10]Of which two have 100 percent foreign ownership.

[11]Of which four have 100 percent foreign ownership.

Table 8.8. Bank Restructuring Measures

	Armenia		Azerbaijan		Belarus		Estonia		Georgia	
	1996	1997	1996	1997[1]	1996	1997[1]	1996	1997	1996	1997[1]
Committee on Bank Restructuring	yes	yes	yes	yes	no	no	no	no	no	no
World Bank Financial Sector Adjustment Loan	no	no	. . .	. . .	yes	no	yes	yes[2]	. . .	. . .
Systemic strategy developed	no	no	no	no	yes	yes	no	no[3]	yes	yes
Deposit insurance in place	no	under consideration	no	no	yes	yes	under preparation	under preparation	no	no
Diagnostic studies undertaken or under way	yes	yes	yes	yes	yes	yes	yes	yes	yes	yes
Operational restructuring measures										
Restrictions on operations of banks	yes	yes	yes	yes	yes	yes	yes	yes	yes	yes
License withdrawals	yes	yes	yes	yes	yes	no	yes	yes	yes	yes
Number of banks	6	3	35	47	4	—	14	6	50	50
Liquidation of banks	yes	yes	yes	yes	yes	yes	. . .	40	yes	yes
Bank mergers and split-offs	yes	yes	yes	yes	yes	no	yes	yes	yes	yes
Number of banks	2	1	4	13	1	—	14	22	7	7
Financial restructuring measures										
Recapitalization	yes	yes[4]	. . .	yes	yes	yes	no	no	no	no
Liquidity injection to banks	no	no	yes	yes	yes	yes	no	no	no	no
Government loan or liability assumption	no	no[5]	yes	yes	yes	yes	. . .	. . .	no	no
Deposit guarantees by government	yes	no	no	no	yes	yes	yes	no	no	no
Existence of asset-management corporation	no	no	no	no	no	no	no	no	no	no
Enterprise restructuring role	. . .	no	. . .	. . .	. . .	no	. . .	. . .	. . .	. . .

	Kazakhstan		Kyrgyz Republic		Latvia		Lithuania		Moldova	
	1996	1997	1996	1997	1996	1997[1]	1996	1997	1996	1997
Committee on Bank Restructuring	yes[6]	yes[6]	yes	yes	no	no	yes	yes	yes[7]	yes
World Bank Financial Sector Adjustment Loan	yes	yes	yes	yes	no	yes[8]	proposed	yes[8]	no	no
Systemic strategy developed	yes	yes	yes	yes	no	yes	proposed	proposed	yes	yes
Deposit insurance in place	no	no	no	under preparation	under preparation	under preparation	yes	yes	no	no
Diagnostic studies undertaken or under way	yes	yes	yes	yes	no	no	proposed	proposed	yes	yes
Operational restructuring measures										
Restrictions on operations of banks	yes	yes	yes	yes	yes	yes	yes	yes	yes	yes
License withdrawals	yes	yes	yes	yes	yes	yes	yes	yes	yes	yes
Number of banks	31	16	5	1	9	9	11	2	2	4
Liquidation of banks	yes	yes[9]	5	1	27	27	—	—	2	4
Bank mergers and split-offs	no	no	yes	yes	yes	yes	no	no	yes	no
Number of banks	3	3	. . .	. . .	2	2	—	. . .	1	. . .
Financial restructuring measures										
Recapitalization	yes	yes	yes	no	partial[10]	partial[10]	yes	yes	yes	yes
Liquidity injection to banks	yes	yes	yes	no	no	no	yes	yes	yes	yes
Government loan/liability assumption	yes	yes	yes	yes	yes	yes	yes	yes	yes[11]	no
Deposit guarantees by government	no	no	yes	no	no	no	yes	yes	no	no
Existence of asset-management corporation	no	no	yes	yes	no	no	yes	yes	no	no
Enterprise restructuring role	. . .	yes	yes	yes	. . .	. . .	planned	yes	. . .	. . .

Table 8.8 *(concluded)*

	Russia		Tajikistan		Turkmenistan		Ukraine		Uzbekistan	
	1996	1997	1996	1997	1996	1997	1996	1997	1996	1997
Committee on bank restructuring	proposed	yes	no	no	no	no	yes	yes	no	yes
World Bank Financial Sector Adjustment Loan	. . .	yes	no	no	no	no	under preparation	no[12]	. . .	yes
Systemic strategy developed	yes	yes	no	no	no	no	no	under preparation	no	yes
Deposit insurance in place	no	under discussion	no	no	no	no	yes	under preparation	no	no
Diagnostic studies undertaken or under way	yes	yes	no	no	yes	yes	yes	yes	no	yes
Operational restructuring measures										
Restrictions on operations on banks	yes	yes	yes	yes	yes	yes	yes	yes	yes	yes
License withdrawal	yes	yes	yes	yes	no	no	yes	yes	yes	no
Number of banks	281	282	. . .	26	. . .	. . .	37	38	1	. . .
Liquidation of banks	yes	yes	1	yes	. . .	. . .	yes	yes	4	1
Bank mergers and split-offs	. . .	. . .[13]	no	. . .	no	no	no	no	no	no
Number of banks	. . .	. . .	. . .	. . .	. . .	. . .	. . .	. . .	. . .	. . .
Financial restructuring measures										
Recapitalization	yes	yes	no	no	no	no	no	no	. . .	yes
Liquidity injection to banks	yes	yes	no	no	no	no	yes	yes	. . .	yes
Government loan or liability assumption	yes[14]	no	no	no	yes[15]	yes[15]	no	no	no	yes
Deposit guarantees by government	partial[16]	partial[17]	no	yes	yes	yes	yes, only Savings Bank	yes, only Savings Bank	People's Bank	People's Bank
Existence of asset-management corporation	no	no	no	no	no	no	no	no	no	no
Enterprise restructuring role	. . .	. . .	. . .	. . .	. . .	. . .	. . .	. . .	. . .	. . .

Sources: Central banks of the Baltic countries, Russia, and other countries of the former Soviet Union.

[1]The data were not submitted for 1997.
[2]Financial Institutions Development Loan. $2.6 million has been disbursed, the remainder of the loan has not been issued.
[3]Bank sector restructuring is in advance stage.
[4]Recapitalization through new owners, rather than directly by government.
[5]The government of Armenia took over the loans to problem state-owned enterprise borrowers by one bank through an asset swap arrangement.
[6]Stopped working in April 1996.
[7]Prudential Bank Supervision Department.
[8]The disbursement of the Financial and Enterprise Sector Restructuring Loan is under way.
[9]As of July 1997, the functions with regard to liquidation of banks as well as regulation and oversight of the liquidation process was transferred to the courts.
[10]State-owned banks only.
[11]Government guarantees.
[12]The loan will be granted only when loan's conditions are met.
[13]The compulsory merger/breakup of banks is not included in the powers of the Central Bank of Russia.
[14]Limited volume.
[15]Government has formally guaranteed some loans to state enterprises.
[16]Government guarantee deposits only in state-owned banks.
[17]Only in savings bank.

Table 8.9. Features of Payment Systems, 1997

	Central Bank Settlement Services and Policy	Distribution of Settlement Accounts	Clearing Times	Large-Value Transfer Systems (LVTS)	Security Transfer Systems
Armenia	Moving to same-day settlement without automatic overdrafts. Information on settlement balances is available promptly under new system.	One account for each bank branch held at head office of central bank.	Delays are being eliminated.	An electronic "all-purpose" system is planned. Telecommunications upgrade is a prerequisite.	A personal-computer-based book-entry system for treasury bills is in operation. A delivery-versus-payment system is planned.
Azerbaijan	Transactions that would overdraw a settlement account are rejected. Information on settlement positions is made available promptly. Settlement is same day in the capital.	One account for each bank branch held with the central bank. A project to rationalize accounts is being discussed.	Clearing times are variable with delays.	No firm plans but discussions have started.	A book-entry system is proposed.
Belarus	Operations on correspondent accounts of banks and non-bank financial organizations at the central bank are effected when there are resources in the account. With a view to supporting liquidity, the National Bank of Belarus (NBB) provides banks with a one-day settlement credit for effective current-day settlements up to a limit collateralized with securities. During an operating day, banks may receive information on the current status of their correspondent account at any time.	Each bank has one correspondent account with the central bank.	Interbank clearing occurs five times per day. There are no delays before funds are released to customers. Settlements are same day.	An electronic system has been introduced for large value, and due payments for interbank settlements on a gross basis in real-time mode. System participants consist of the NBB, banks, and nonbank financial organizations. The operator of the system is the "Belarussian Interbank Settlement Center" state enterprise.	A system of settlements for securities transactions using the "delivery-versus-payment" principle is planned.

Estonia	Settlement is end of day after interbank trading of funds. Any potential overdrafts at settlement are avoided by rejecting payments to the amount of the potential overdraft.	Banks have one central settlement account.	Clearing is generally prompt. Customers may experience delays if the central bank rejects payments. In this case banks are required to carry out the payment order within two days.	The central bank is planning a new real-time gross settlement (RTGS) system. Currently high-value payments are made across a paper-based gross settlement system or an all-purpose electronic funds transfer system.	There is a book-entry system that supports delivery versus payment.
Georgia	The central bank does not give automatic overdrafts. Settlement is end of day. Banks do not receive information on settlement positions promptly.	Banks have one settlement account.	Clearing times are slow and unpredictable.	An LVTS based on RTGS is planned. It will be nationwide and run by the central bank.	There is no book-entry securities transfer system.
Kazakhstan	The central bank does not allow overdrafts. Information to help liquidity management is promptly available in the capital but not nationwide. There are plans to develop an intraday liquidity facility.	Most banks (96 percent) now hold one account with the central bank, and the remainder will move to one account soon.	Clearing times for payments within the capital are prompt and predictable.	LVTS are carried on an RTGS-like electronic system. The system allows for large-value transfers in real-time.	A book-entry system for transfers of treasury bills exists and is linked to the gross settlement system.
Kyrgyz Republic	There are no automatic overdrafts. Banks are required to access funds in the inter-bank market or to use the Lombard facility. Banks are provided with information on account positions promptly. Settlement is same day.	Banks have one central settlement account.	Clearing times are slow and unpredictable. There are delays in interprovince payments.	There is a paper-based system for processing large-value payments in the capital. There are plans, but no timetable, for an RTGS system.	A book-entry system for transfer of securities is operating.

Table 8.9 *(concluded)*

	Central Bank Settlement Services and Policy	Distribution of Settlement Accounts	Clearing Times	Large-Value Transfer Systems (LVTS)	Security Transfer Systems
Latvia	No automatic overdrafts are given.	Banks have one central settlement account.	Clearing times are prompt and predictable.	A dedicated RTGS system is planned. At present, high-value payments are processed either using a paper-based system or using an all-purpose electronic system.	A book-entry system for transfer of securities is operating.
Lithuania	No automatic overdrafts are given. Settlement is same day and banks are given information on account positions promptly.	Banks have one central settlement account.	Clearing times are prompt and predictable.	A national electronic RTGS system is planned.	A book-entry transfer system is in operation. It is to be linked to the RTGS system.
Moldova	No automatic overdrafts are given. Banks are given information on settlement account positions promptly.	Banks have one central settlement account.	Clearing times are prompt and predictable.	There are no plans at present for a specialized system.	A book-entry system for transfer of securities is operating.
Russia	Overnight overdraft is available for selected banks. Settlement became same day in March 1997. Information on settlement balances became available to banks in March 1997. The Lombard facility cannot be used to cover for end-of-day liquidity shortfalls. Effective June 1998, one-day and interday collateralized overdrafts are available to all banks within individual limits calculated	Commercial banks maintain settlement accounts in regional divisions of the central bank at the location of a bank and its branches. There are moves to consolidate accounts. Major banks are consolidating accounts with the central bank at a regional level.	Processing is done within 24 hours within cities; clearing times longer and variable otherwise.	Plans for the establishment of an RTGS system are being finalized. A fully operating system should begin functioning in Moscow within a year.	There is a paperless securities transfer system. Links to the proposed RTGS system are being discussed. The current system supports delivery versus payment but funds are not available to payees until the next day.

	on the basis of the market value of the bank's government securities portfolio.				
Tajikistan	Overdrafts are not permitted. Information on account positions is not available to banks to allow efficient liquidity management.	Commercial banks hold settlement accounts with the central bank branches in each region. No rationalization is planned.	Clearing times are not prompt or predictable.	There has been some discussion of an LVTS but plans are not firm. Telecommunications appear inadequate.	A book-entry transfer system has been discussed.
Turkmenistan	Automatic overdrafts are given. Information on account positions is not available to banks to allow efficient liquidity management.	Commercial banks have one account for each branch at each regional clearinghouse.	Clearing times vary from one to five days.	An electronic national system is planned to carry small- and large-value payments. There is special processing of paper-based large-value payment orders.	There is a book-entry system for treasury bills.
Ukraine	No automatic overdrafts are given. Any access to credit is at penalty rates. Information is available to allow banks to manage their liquidity positions within the day.	Some banks have centralized their settlement accounts, but not all.	Clearing times are prompt and predictable.	Large value items are carried on an electronic system. The system is not a specialized high-value system. An RTGS system is planned.	There is a book-entry system that is linked to the electronic payment system.
Uzbekistan	No automatic overdrafts are given. Banks receive information on account positions to allow efficient liquidity management. Settlement is same day.	Commercial bank branches hold settlement accounts with each regional branch of the central bank. There are plans to consolidate branch accounts at the regional level.	Clearing times are prompt and predictable.	Large value items are carried on an electronic system. The system is not a specialized high-value system.	There is an operational book-entry transfer system. This operates on a delivery-versus-payment basis.

Source: IMF.

Table 8.10. Central Bank Accounting Reforms, 1997

	Current Information Source for Policymakers	New Chart of Accounts and International Accounting Standards (IAS) Financial Statements	International Assessment of Accounting Reforms	Future Reform Issues Requiring Technical Assistance
Armenia	Monetary and financial reports are based on a new chart of accounts.	The new chart was introduced in 1996. Financial statement format is consistent with IAS. Accrual-based profit measurement is used.	The first IAS external audit of the end-1995 accounts was unqualified, and a full qualified audit opinion was obtained for 1996. Annual IAS audits are ongoing.	Development of internal control systems and risk-based audit assessment, auditing computer developments, and introduction of budgetary control and costing systems should all be incorporated.
Azerbaijan	Monetary and financial reports are based on a new chart of accounts.	The new chart was introduced in 1997. The new formatted balance sheet is available for internal use at the central bank. Accrual basis accounting has been adopted except for interest on loans.	An IAS external audit was conducted for the 1996 year-end accounts and received an unqualified opinion.	Improvement of accounting procedures for specific activities and definition of rules for adoption of new chart of accounts by commercial banks are recommended.
Belarus	Monetary and financial reports are based on a new chart of accounts.	The new chart was introduced in 1996. Financial statement format is consistent with IAS. Accrual-based profit measurement has been accepted.	An IAS external audit of end-1996 accounts received unqualified opinion.	Development of procedures for operations in the securities and exchange markets is suggested.
Estonia	Monetary and financial data are based on a new chart of accounts format.	A new chart was adopted, but recording is done using the old chart and then converted to new-format reports. Profits are measured on an accrual basis and financial statement format is consistent with IAS.	There are ongoing annual IAS audits. Unqualified opinions have been received for the last four years.	Installation of new accounting information systems is recommended, with a new general ledger and chart of accounts incorporated over the next two to three years. Cooperation is suggested with commercial banks in the development of a new chart of accounts for banks.

Georgia	Monetary and financial reports are based on a new chart of accounts.	The new chart was introduced in 1996 for summary level reporting and financial statement preparation. Financial statement format is consistent with IAS. Accrual-based profit measurement is in place.	First IAS audit of 1996 accounts resulted in an unqualified opinion of end-year balances. Annual IAS audits are ongoing.	New accounting software should be installed, and development of detailed operating procedures enacted.
Kazakhstan	Monetary data and financial information are based on a new chart of accounts.	The new chart was introduced in 1997, incorporating IAS and income accrual principles measurement. Financial statements are based on IAS format.	The first diagnostic IAS external audit was held in 1995. A subsequent audit of 1996 accounts gave a qualified opinion on the basis of differing accounting methods for gold and foreign currency reserves.	Integration of accounting software and subsystems, documentation of accounting procedures, elaboration of standards, and instructions for commercial banks are all recommended.
Kyrgyz Republic	Monetary and financial reports are based on a new chart of accounts.	The new chart was introduced in 1997, incorporating IAS and accrual-based profit measurement. In-house developed accounting software has been installed. Financial statements for 1997 will be based on the new chart.	A diagnostic IAS external audit was undertaken in 1995, and continuing audits were held thereafter. A qualified opinion was received for end-1996 accounts.	Development or finalization of detailed procedures for operations in foreign exchange, gold, securities, and credits should be undertaken. Accounting and consolidation principles for commercial banks that promote future development of internal procedures by banks themselves are suggested.
Latvia	Monetary and financial data are based on a new chart of accounts.	The new chart was introduced in 1993. Financial statements are prepared according to IAS, and profits are measured on an accrual basis.	"Clean" IAS audit opinions have been given since 1994 accounts, with ongoing annual IAS audits.	Fine-tuning commercial bank compliance with IAS should occur, and guidelines for improving internal control systems at commercial banks should be enacted.

Table 8.10 ***(concluded)***

	Current Information Source for Policymakers	New Chart of Accounts and International Accounting Standards (IAS) Financial Statements	International Assessment of Accounting Reforms	Future Reform Issues Requiring Technical Assistance
Lithuania	Monetary and financial data are based on a new chart of accounts.	The new chart was introduced in 1993. Financial statements are prepared according to IAS. Profits are measured on an accrual basis.	"Clean" IAS audit opinions have been given since 1995, with ongoing annual IAS audits.	Changes to central bank strategic management information systems are recommended.
Moldova	Monetary and financial data are based on a new chart of accounts.	The new chart was introduced in 1995. Financial statements are prepared according to IAS, and accrual basis was adopted from January 1, 1998.	An IAS external audit has not yet been undertaken.	Refinements to chart of accounts, implementation of rules and procedures to make national accounting standards consistent with IAS.
Russia	Monetary and financial reports are based on "old" chart of accounts, and have been modified for new activities.	The new chart was introduced in January 1998, but does not adopt income accrual principles. IAS-consistent policies have been adopted for foreign exchange accounting.	IAS diagnostic audits have been completed for 1993, 1994, and 1995. An IAS audit has not been undertaken because it is not required under Russian law.	Development of principles for uniform transition to accrual-based standards by central bank and commercial banks is suggested.
Tajikistan	Monetary and financial reports are based on the "old" chart of accounts, and have been modified for new activities.	A new chart is under consideration, and accounting policies and financial statement format is yet to be determined. Profits are measured on a cash basis.	An IAS external audit has not yet been undertaken.	An intensive implementation program to develop a new chart of accounts and IAS-based practices will be required.

Turkmenistan	Monetary and financial reports are based on the old chart of accounts, which has been modified for new activities.	A new chart representing a modernization but not a departure from the former chart of accounts of the Soviet Union was introduced in March 1998. National accounting standards require conformity with IAS.	An IAS external audit has not yet been undertaken. A new chart was, however, developed with assistance from an international accounting firm.	Computerization issues associated with implementation of the new chart of accounts should be undertaken. Further documentation of regulations to ensure IAS-based practices are understood and widely practiced is recommended.
Ukraine	As of January 1, 1998 monetary and financial reports have been based on a new chart of accounts and are submitted by all of Ukraine's banks.	The new chart of accounts based on IAS and the accrual principle, as well as a new package of financial and statistical reports, became effective on January 1, 1998.	An IAS external audit of 1995 accounts resulted in a qualified opinion. An external audit by an international audit company on the 1996 consolidated balance sheet concluded that statements were consistent with existing legislation. An external audit for 1997 is nearing completion. External audits are expected to continue.	Ongoing reform of central bank accounting and internal audit systems is recommended, as is commercial bank accounting reform to adopt IAS.
Uzbekistan	Monetary and financial reporting is based on a new chart.	A new chart has been introduced and is broadly consistent with IAS. Financial statement format is still under development.	An IAS external audit has not yet been undertaken. Some evaluation has been made of commercial bank reporting on a diagnostic basis.	Ongoing development of recording procedures and financial reporting format under IAS is recommended.

Source: IMF.